T0171467

"A wonderful book for anyone who has tried to 'go it alone' spiritually – this book will keep you company, lift your spirits and make you laugh."

Victoria Moran, Author of *Creating a Charmed Life*

"One of my life's opportunities (otherwise known as a sharp stick in the spiritual eye) is to become more sovereign, to belong more to myself, to trust myself more. I was so delighted to read Kaite's fresh and tantalizing take on bringing more faith and self-trust into my soul life. I highly recommend this book."

Jennifer Louden, Author of *The Woman's Comfort Book* and *The Life Organizer*, www.jenniferlouden.com

---

"Kaite McGrew has crafted a gorgeous and important work in Sovereign Soul by providing an understanding and experience of spirituality that is larger and more vast than we are and simultaneously large and vast within. Most of us veer toward one or the other. We need both. And it is to this that she writes, calls, and compels. A blending of deeply powerful prose and practical application, Kaite offers our souls what they most long for and deeply need. Listen to her and in the process, hear your own sovereign soul speak."

Ronna Detrick, M.Div., Writer & Spiritual Director, www.ronnadetrick.com

---

"Beautifully written and full of practical strategies, this book is a must-read for any woman trying to build a reliable spiritual practice on her own"

Sonia Miller, Best-Selling Author of *The Attraction Distraction: Why the Law of Attraction Isn't Working for You and How to Get Results - Finally!* and Founder of www.SuccessForTheSoul.com

The

Sovereign Soul

The
Sovereign Soul

A Spiritual-but-Not-Religious Woman's Guide to Living a Soul-Centered Life

Kaite McGrew

Illustrations by Geoffrey Mundon

ISBN: 978-1-4525-5569-0 (sc)
ISBN: 978-1-4525-5568-3 (e)

Balboa Press books may be ordered through booksellers or by contacting:

Balboa Press
A Division of Hay House
1663 Liberty Drive
Bloomington, IN 47403
www.balboapress.com
1-(877) 407-4847

Printed in the United States of America

Balboa Press rev. date: 11/09/2012

Table of Contents

Introduction i

A Letter from Your Sovereign Soul 1

Becoming Willing 9

Making Room for Your Sovereign Soul 26

Making Time for Your Sovereign Soul 58

Cultivating Profound Privacy 87

Creating a Consistent Spiritual Practice 109

Building Your Tribe 147

Stepping Into Service 164

What To Do When You Get Stuck 173

A Few Last Thoughts 183

Introduction

Welcome. There are a lot of reasons you may have picked up this book. Maybe something about it resonated with you. When you looked at it, you felt something, some energy, some excitement, maybe even recognition. You read the words "Sovereign Soul" and you may have heard it, faintly at first, but then getting louder. You weren't even sure what it meant - what is a "Sovereign Soul" exactly? - but somehow when you read the words, they felt familiar to you, intriguing, and somehow strangely satisfying. Some part of you, deep in your bones, recognized *yourself* in those words "Sovereign Soul" even as you read them silently to yourself a few times.

There's a chance that you recognized yourself in those words, exactly as you are today. But there's an even greater chance that you recognized the <u>You</u> that you came here to be; the version of yourself that you keep longing for, but somehow never quite get around to becoming. You know the one I am talking about. Sometimes you see her on the street; she walks right by you and you recognize her. Sometimes you see her in a character that you identify with on TV. Or maybe you're reading a particularly powerful piece of spiritual work, or listening to a powerful speaker, and you can actually hear her voice inside of you, urging you to pay attention, listen closely.

Sometimes you dream about her, and when she shows up in your dreams, (either as you or with you), you feel more energized, more powerful and more alive than you've ever felt before. It's distinct and joyful and it stays with you for days after the dream. You can remember what it was like to be her, even if only for that short while.

Other times she can be irritating, when you want something to be easy, when you want to fit in, when you want someone around to do that "heavy lifting" for you, but there she is, independent as ever, and pointing out all the things you are trying hard not to notice.

She is persuasive and she can be persistent, this part of you. But she has to be. She is your Sovereign Soul and she has a purpose. She came here with a job to do. Her job is to deepen and strengthen your connection to God. She is your Divinity. She is your Highest Self. Your Sovereign Soul is the deepest, most connected, most powerful part of who you are, and if you picked up this book, then it is finally time to actually welcome her into your life, instead of just dreaming about her. Your Sovereign Soul has been in love with you all of your life. Not just any love, but a deep and abiding love, a sustaining love - a Great and Mighty Love. And if you are reading this now, chances are you are ready to fall for her too. You are finally ready to love her back, the way that she loves you.

This book is that love story. It is the story of how you embarked upon the journey home and with each step along the way fell more and more deeply in love with your own beautiful Soul. It is the story of how you finally came to really know her, and the more you knew her, the more you delighted in her. The more you came to rely upon her, the more you trusted her. It is the story of how she became your best friend and your constant companion, and in doing so began to direct your life in new and beautiful ways. It is a story about trust, and faith and devotion. This book is a love story.

This book is also a guidebook. Throughout its pages you will find what I hope will be useful information, with powerful but practical strategies and a generous helping of inspiration all designed to help you discover and come to know the most beautiful part of who you are and find your way home. The quality of your journey will depend entirely upon what you bring to it. I encourage you to take what is useful, discard what is not, and try everything that appeals to you. This is an exploration. Your journey into the heart of yourself, your passionate love affair with your own Divinity - this is the greatest adventure – this is where the treasure lies! This is *why* you are you.

I wrote this book in answer to my own prayers, to keep me company and to guide me on my own journey home. I wrote this book for smart, soulful women who long to deeply know themselves spiritually but struggle to do so without the structure or support of an organized religion. I wrote this book for all women who identify as independent spiritual seekers, women who live lives of faith, but faith undefined. I wrote this book for women who have not yet shaped their lives to support their faith. If you have been unable yet to collect energy around your spiritual journey, to bring that journey to the forefront of your life – if you think you have to choose between an organized religion and a hit-or-miss spiritual life, then I wrote this book for you.

This book is not the territory. It is not even the map. This book does not have the answers but it does have the questions. It is your Self, your own beautiful Sovereign Soul, who has the answers you seek. This book can encourage you and keep you company as you open yourself to your Soul – as you learn how to ask the questions and how to hear the answers. It is my hope that you will use this opportunity to explore and to discover your own Sovereign Soul and to fall as deeply in love with her as she is with you.

This book will support you in cultivating and expanding the qualities within you that strengthen your connection with your Sovereign Soul. The journey will be an expansion of who you know yourself to be, and what you believe yourself to be capable of. The territory may feel unfamiliar, but it is a journey home, and your Sovereign Soul will walk with you every step of the way. In her you have the most trustworthy advisor and most beloved friend. If you open to your Soul, if you let her work her magic on you, you will come to truly know this friend, and when you do, you cannot help but fall deeply in love with her.

Your own Sovereign Soul is the most beautiful, captivating thing you will ever witness if you let yourself. When you make your relationship with your Soul a priority, you will open the door to that deep, abiding, completely trustworthy presence that is always with you. This is the love that every seeker seeks. This is the experience of the Divine the seeker craves. Every other relationship in your life will be colored by the beauty of your love affair with your own Sovereign Soul. Every aspect of your life will be enriched, enlivened, and enlightened by that love.

Before you can really love someone, you must come to know them deeply. To do that, you will need to create the conditions and opportunities for that to happen. And you start with yourself - you start by preparing yourself to receive her. So let's begin.

Imagine if your Sovereign Soul was able to write you a letter...

A Letter from
Your Sovereign Soul

Dear Beloved Seeker,

There is so much that I want to show you, that I want to share with you. I have been waiting a long time for you to invite me into your life. More than anything I want to support, inspire and guide you as you grow into the beautiful being that you came here to be. You are wonderful and you have always been wonderful. I can see where you have been and my greatest joy is to be with you as you fulfill your promise in this life.

There are some things that you can pay attention to - things that you can do to make your journey easier and your connection with me stronger. If you give each of these elements your attention and your energy, if you apply these concepts to the living of your life, then you will be creating the most ideal opportunities for me to support you and to accompany you on your journey.

In return I promise to enrich your life on every level and in ways that you could never have imagined. I promise to inspire and delight you as often as you will let me and I promise to comfort and guide you when you feel lost or disconnected. I love you unconditionally, as God loves you, because I am the part of you that has never left God, the Divinity that resides within you.

Every love you have known – the love of a child, a parent, a spouse, a pet, a dear friend – every one of these loves is but a fragment of the love that I hold for you. Each one is just a taste of what the fullness of unconditional love is from my vantage point. It is almost impossible for you to fully experience the breadth and depth of my love for you from your human space/time experience. Instead you will be given opportunities to experience more and more aspects of this love as you prepare your heart to receive it. You will begin to see it everywhere, and you will recognize it in the love you experience from elements of your life – human and non-human, even aspects of nature that surround you. You will begin to feel my love and God's love more and more frequently from more and more sources as you begin to allow me into your life.

This is the sole purpose of my presence in your life – to allow you to meet the world with and through your own Divinity. The more you allow me expression in your life, the more you receive my presence into your heart, the more able you are to meet life from these higher aspects, and to bless the world in so doing.

There are some things that you can do to make this happen more fully and more quickly. Each of these things will create greater and greater conditions and opportunities for me to express myself in your life and for you to receive me in your heart. Each of these things will open the door just a little bit more to the Divinity within you and your ability to access it more fully and to share it more deeply.

I know that you sometimes feel alone with your faith, and that you sometimes lose your way because you believe yourself to be on your own, but you are not. I am always here. I am always with you. I surround you with my love at all times. I am always here to serve you and protect you and guide you. The more you come to know me, the more you will learn to trust me and to trust your connection with me. Over time you will find that building that connection, strengthening our bond, will become central in your life and will inform your choices every day. I will become your primary relationship, and all other relationships will be enriched because of ours. The more you love me, the more I will be able to lift and support all of the loves in your life.

Until then, there are some things that you can do to strengthen that connection and deepen your ability to experience my presence in your life.

Become Willing

First I ask that you become willing and receptive. Allow yourself to be curious, and eager for deeper connection, broader understanding and fuller expression. Make yourself available to the adventure, approaching it with "beginner's mind" – focused but full of wonder. This is exactly the mindset most conducive to falling in love, and it is exactly this mindset that best welcomes me into your life.

I'm asking that you be willing to let your faith change you and change the way that you do things. I'm asking you to try things before you dismiss them, and that you be honest with yourself about how you've been living until now, and willing to see what needs changing, if anything. I'm asking you to let me change you, impact and shape you. I'm asking you to trust me and to be vulnerable to me. And I am asking that you commit to doing that so that I can work in and through you in your life. I promise you will not be disappointed or hurt by placing your trust in me. I am the highest, wisest and most compassionate aspect of your being and you can trust me completely to offer you only that which serves your highest good and the good of all concerned.

Make Room for Me

Please invite me into the physical environments of your life. Welcome me into your home, into your work spaces, your creative spaces, and your vehicles. Make room for me and celebrate me in all the spaces that you inhabit.

Seek out and create the elements that remind you of me, and that connect you to me as you go through your day. View all the places in your life through my eyes – eliminate what forms a barrier between us, and emphasize what forms a connection between us. By welcoming me physically into your life, by allowing your physical spaces to support and enrich your connection with me, you let our bond cross the bridge from the purely energetic to the manifest material. You allow yourself to engage with me physically, and to bring my influence to the wholeness of your life. This is incredibly powerful, and deepens your understanding of my role in your life and my ability to serve you in everything.

Make Time for Me

In order for our connection to deepen and our bond to strengthen, you will need to make me your priority. This cannot be avoided. I know that your life seems to move in fits and starts. I know that sometimes you lose the thread of it, and it seems chaotic or perhaps out of your control. I know many people and many activities lay claim to your time and your attention. What I need you to know is that I am what you most need. In all things and at all times, with no exception. I am what you most need. It is time now for you to put me at the center of your life and allow yourself to align with me before you seek to approach any other task. Your various roles in life (mother, wife, employee, sister, daughter, citizen, shopper, caregiver) will all be empowered and illuminated when you approach them from the foundation of your perfect alignment with me.

Align your priorities with mine. Renew your commitment to giving your relationship with me ample time to develop. Without that time, you cannot hope to know me better than you do, and you cannot fully discover what I offer you. I am asking you to look deeply at the nature of time and your relationship to it. I am asking you to evaluate how you spend your time in terms of how it impacts your connection with me. I am asking you to begin to make the small but significant choices that support your faith and your ability to know me deeply.

On your journey you will learn to identify the various qualities of time spent in spiritual pursuits, and how to find, craft, invent and maximize the time that you have. As you make your way, you will begin to develop a new relationship with time itself, and with your own sense of commitment to your spiritual path. And as you begin to master your relationship with time, you will find that your path will shift from a challenging one to a compelling one. And I will be right there with you. The more time and attention you can offer me, the more I will be able to support you in these changes, and less effort they will require. This transformation will build upon itself, as you gain momentum. But you have to give it time.

Observe Profound Privacy

The more your life becomes a life of devotion, the more you will find that you require sustained privacy in which to develop. As you bring yourself closer to the Divine within you, you will find that our relationship is an intensely intimate one. By opening yourself fully to me, you will find that there is nothing you can conceal and much that you will reveal that is just between you, and I, and God. That is the nature of the work that we will be doing together.

As much as you need the society of other like-minded seekers you will also need time alone with me, and a strong sense of boundaries around that time. Your open heart is vulnerable and in a state of flux. Much of your exploration will need to be done in a sacred protected space where you can be alone with me and feel free to experience that connection honestly.

I am asking you to look deeply at privacy, boundaries and solitude. As you do, you will begin to craft an intuitive sense of how much of it you need to feel free and to feel safe, and how to determine when you need it. You'll explore how to protect yourself emotionally and spiritually during more vulnerable times, and how to recognize when you are overstepping your own capacity for sharing on a spiritual level. By cultivating both a deep respect for your journey and the profound privacy it requires, you will create a safe and open space for an authentically intimate relationship with yourself, with me and with God.

Build a Consistent Spiritual Practice

Because you do not approach me from the base of an organized religion, you will need to find or create your own ways to commemorate and celebrate your spiritual life. Every organized religion contains within it deeply symbolic traditions and rituals enacted over time, deepening in significance each time they are repeated. All spiritual life can benefit from a climate rich with tradition and ritual but you will meet an additional challenge in creating that climate for yourself outside of an organized faith.

Although there are many beautiful and powerful traditions and rituals in the wisdom teachings of all the cultures, it is easy for the independent seeker to become overwhelmed and distracted by the sheer volume and the potential for contradictions when experimenting with a variety of traditions from a variety of sources.

I'm asking you to bring your attention to finding and creating rituals and traditions that feel right for you now, and that you can count on to support you in your journey. I am asking you to bring these traditions and rituals together, so they strengthen the impact of one another, and your bond with me. I will be guiding you, offering you new information, inspiring you as you weave together a solid spiritual practice to support you as you move through your days, weeks, months and years. I will work with you to help you discern elements of the practice that are appropriate for you as they become appropriate. The practice will evolve and grow and begin to become self-supporting, simply part of how you interact with life. Slowly but surely, you will fine tune it with your focus and your spiritual practice will shift from being haphazard and scattered to grounded, cohesive and whole. In this way, you will be able to develop your commitment and enrich your life more fully with my presence.

Build a Tribe You Can Trust

Once you've developed the basic structures to support your consistent, authentic spiritual practice, I encourage you to find or build a tribe. Your tribe does not have to subscribe to all of your spiritual beliefs in order to support your growth spiritually. They simply need to be a collection of like-minded individuals that share at least some areas of common intellectual and spiritual ground. And they will have to respect your individuality and support your intentions for yourself.

Aligning yourself with a tribe that respects your individual faith can be a very powerful experience. Even if they do not know that they are functioning as a tribe for you, they can still serve as one. The tribe can protect and inspire you by creating opportunities for exploration and a much needed sense of stability in an ever changing world.

Step into Service

When you have developed your practice and connected with a tribe that supports your spiritual exploration, I will ask you to look again deeply at your faith in terms of your ability to serve. Your deepening connection with me is not simply to bless you, but to bless the world. As you grow spiritually, so you develop your ability to serve life, to serve the world and to serve Divinity itself. This is a fundamental aspect of all spiritual life, and a necessary and beautiful shift – when the seeker becomes the world server. I will ask you to complete that circuit, to find ways to bless life and to love and serve life as I bless and love and serve you.

These are the practical, beautiful steps in your journey to union with me, my beloved seeker. No matter what, I will be there always, to guide and protect you as you take them. Trust me, and come to know me, that you may love me as I love you – completely and without reservation. Call on me often, and open yourself to my influence. I will never let you down.

Love,

Your Beloved Sovereign Soul

Chapter One
Becoming Willing

So we begin. The first step in opening to your Sovereign Soul is to become willing to do that. So, how exactly do we do that? What can you, as an independent seeker, right from where you are now, do to foster your own willingness and become fully receptive to your own Soul? How can you allow her influence most fully into your life?

Observe

The first and possibly most important step for you to take is to become completely conscious about your current structure. You do have a structure to your days, and weeks, and months, that exists right now, even without your having consciously decided upon its components. Becoming aware of that structure with clarity and honesty is a powerful step in the right direction. Right now it isn't about judging your current structure, or marshalling your "self-improvement" forces or overturning the invisible priorities that currently govern your days and nights. Right now, you are only looking for clarity – you want to try to see things for what they are, free of judgment and free of any need to force any shifts that you may not be ready for just yet.

The things that we do with our time, we do because they are comfortable for us, and because they match up to our current version of who we are, or at least, who we present ourselves to be. These "bones" of our lives are not something we are eager to upend, or dissolve with a quick maneuver. Although it is true that sometimes life will upend itself, on its own, we individuals are rarely in any hurry to do it ourselves. So for a week or so, the first step to your willingness is just to commit to two things – to observe and to record your observations. You will want to study the "bones" of your life – the routines, habits and boundaries that you have set up for yourself – the millions of tiny rituals that have settled comfortably into your life and attend you every moment of every day. Don't judge. Don't fix. Just observe.

Record

The second step is to record your observations. You don't need to have this conversation with anyone else in your life, or let anyone know what you are doing. Just get a journal and begin to record your observations. If it is helpful, you can also record your feeling states during these different components of your daily structure. Again, you aren't judging those states. You aren't making commentary on the rightness or wrongness of your feelings. You are just observing the structure of your day (what you have disciplined yourself to do, over time) and how that structure impacts your state of mind, your state of heart.

You can take your time with this part of the process. It can take some time to observe a pattern and to realize that it is, in fact, a pattern or habit. Often we do things because we think they have to be done that way, when in fact we have simply chosen to do them that way. It can take some time and some cultivated awareness to make that distinction - so give yourself the time you need to let your awareness broaden and deepen. You are in no hurry.

Reserve Judgment

Reserving judgment and simply noting what you witness will develop your ability to be comfortable with the stance of the detached observer. This is not a position that we take often, so any opportunity to practice is welcome. Usually we leap almost immediately from an observation to an opinion about that observation. If you can take your time right now just getting comfortable with the sensation of being a detached observer, then you deepen your ability to hold that space more often and for longer periods of time. Holding that space becomes part of the structure of your day, and one of the foundational pieces on your journey to expanded willingness and allowing the full expression of your Sovereign Soul.

Practice holding the position of the neutral observer, as you would practice holding a yoga position. Bring your awareness and your intention to it. If you feel yourself starting to lose conscious awareness as the observer, gently bring yourself back into that desired awareness. If you feel yourself starting to get caught up in a judgment or emotional response to anything you are observing (either in the moment, or later when you are recording the event), again, just gently bring yourself back to a detached and neutral stance. Take your time to practice approaching your life from this stance, without any need to change it or fix it or comment upon it or embellish it or hold onto it. Right now you have only one mission: to become aware of the structures you have built into your life and to observe how those structures make you feel when they are a reinforced.

Explore

When you are ready, the next step for you is going to be about shifting out of a purely observational role and more into the role of the explorer. You will continue to observe, but you will also be experimenting with small changes to the way you do things. You aren't trying to shock yourself into a whole new reality, by the way. You are just looking for small areas of give and take that are already built into the structure of your day, and then applying small increments of intention to those points. Think of it as wiggle room. Because you have been carefully observing and noting how doing certain things in certain ways makes you feel, start with those observations and let them point you in the right direction.

If there are things that you do, and ways that you do them that deepen your feelings of connectedness to the Divine, then see where else you can do similar things in similar ways in order to increase the time you spend in that state of connectedness. If there are certain things you do every day that habitually make you feel disconnected or overwhelmed, then those would be places where you can do some journaling around what small changes in the routine/ritual you can experiment with to increase connectedness and decrease overwhelm.

This, too, does not need to be something that you rush through. You aren't out to fix anything broken, or purge anything toxic, necessarily. Instead, you are more like an archeologist in the landscape of your day, looking for signs of your Soul. Your Sovereign Soul exists completely intact and whole, beneath the surface of your daily life as it looks to you today. You, like the archeologist, are settled comfortably on the surface of your life, and gently, very gently, with a soft brush, you are removing the earth around it. You are slowly, patiently uncovering the mystery and wonder that is the city of your beautiful Sovereign Soul just beneath the surface of your life. You are right on time and there is no need to rush. No need to force or push or effort with anything. You can let it come, on its own. The territory will sometimes challenge you and in response to those challenges you will find new disciplines called forth from within you. But you do not need to implement any harsh or rigid efforts. Right now you are simply exploring, guided as much by your curiosity as by your intention. You are opening. Surrender.

Be Curious

Curiosity is one of your greatest allies. And, truthfully, aren't you curious to know who you are when you are *really being who you came here to be*? Aren't you curious to know how things appear to you from that vantage point? How you respond to those things when you are really being that version of yourself?

It is the tantalizing elixir of curiosity that beckons you down this path, and curiosity that will eventually call forth those hidden disciplines. For now it is enough to approach it all with the patience and attention of the archeologist, unearthing a great but hidden treasure. You can let the treasure itself show you where to dig, and how fast to dig, and how carefully to dig. Your faith, both in the Divine and in your own whole and complete Sovereign Soul, will light your way and inform your exploration. All you have to do is allow it.

Enlighten Your Load

So far in your journey you have observed, you have recorded, and you have explored. There have been small but conscious shifts that you've made in your routines. There have probably been some that happened almost automatically once you brought your awareness to the way you were doing things. You have practiced opening yourself to the treasure, letting it inform you where and how to seek it. With each approach, you've examined one small portion of what living your life is about, one unique angle from which to approach the Divine and one small aspect of the full expression of your Sovereign Soul.

There may be some part of you that has been exhausted by your efforts or by the sheer exposure that that level of attention can bring to the mind and the heart. You may be wondering, at this point, whether the whole journey home will be this deliberate, this painstaking.

The masters and the mystics speak of the state of "enlightenment" and one always gets the impression that this state is one that requires a lifetime of discipline to achieve. If you choose to understand it that way, then you position "enlightenment" as a destination, rather than a journey. Just contemplating a journey to such a lofty destination is enough to frighten off many seekers. When "enlightenment" becomes a goal, living a life designed to reach that goal can feel like a trial.

I would like to suggest an alternate way to hold the concept of enlightenment. What if enlightenment is the gradual increase in both the quantity and the quality of "light" that you bring to your journey? What if it is not a destination at all, but instead, a process? What if enlightenment *is the path itself*? If that were the case, how would enlightenment look to you today, right now, from where you are this minute?

Pray

Your Sovereign Soul is already there, dear seeker. Your Soul is both the journey and the destination. She does not need of any fixing or finding. All that she requires is the room - the opportunity - to express herself as often as you can let that happen. You will not lapse into a state of detached bliss and lose your grip on reality. You will not alienate the world and find yourself marooned on your own island of spiritual reverie. You will not lose sight of what has been important to you in the past and somehow forget to take your responsibilities seriously. None of your greatest fears will come to be.

It is true that there will probably be things about your journey that will startle you or intimidate you. You may become uncomfortable or afraid from time to time. That much is true. But you will come to these things in their own good time and when you have reached a stage in your development when you are ready for them. So do not be afraid to let your Sovereign Soul express herself whenever and however you can.

If you allow it, the day will come when almost everything you do will be a prayer. You will feel the constant presence of the Divine in your life, in yourself and in others more often than not. It will become rare and unfamiliar to find yourself disconnected from your Divinity, and when it happens you will notice the disconnection immediately. Then you will know that you have allowed your life to become a Soul-centered life. For now your only task is to make as much of your day a living prayer as you possibly can.

Let the way you wake up be a prayer. Let the way you eat be a prayer. Let the way you listen to others be a prayer. Let the way you care for those you love be a prayer. Let the way that you care for your body be a prayer. Let the way you move your body be a prayer. Let the way that you interact with others out in the world, on the freeway, in the market, at the doctor's office be a prayer. Let the way that you do your work be a prayer. Let the way that you study be a prayer. Let the way that you close your day, and the way that you lay down to rest be a prayer. Pray with your life, pray with your whole life.

Try not to become rigid in your habits and manners around your activities, but recognize instead, that prayer is a living, fluid, call-and-response activity. As you become truly present, you will become as receptive as you are expressive, and your way of doing things will vary as you receive and respond to the call of your Sovereign Soul. So let your ways be informed by the state of your being and by your own presence of mind. Relax. Rejoice. Receive.

Trust

For a long time now, you have probably been completely ignoring the call of your Sovereign Soul. You may even have been actively suppressing it so as not to feel the discomfort of not having answered it. As you begin to work consciously in this arena, it may feel counter-intuitive to stop suppressing that call and instead to actively go in search of it. Allow for the discomfort, at least for the time being.

If you allow for it, you will find that you need do little more than simply wait for the discomfort to pass. So much of the way you have approached your Soul has simply been learned habit and will take a little while to become unlearned. If you can hold your ground and wait for it, if you can stay steady, through the discomfort, those habits will usually dissipate of their own accord.

This approach carries with it an even stronger directive to your personality; it reminds you that you can trust your Sovereign Soul. You are not wrestling a lazy mind or a stubborn heart into submission. You are not forcing yourself into any sort of penance or guilty servitude. You are resisting nothing. Instead you are actively demonstrating your faith in the rightness of what your Soul demands. By holding your ground and waiting, you affirm the natural order of your Sovereign Soul's presence in the very center of your life.

By not resisting the feelings of discomfort and actively leaving yourself open to this natural order, you create a space. A space between the feeling and your response to the feeling. A space between the event and the outcome. A space inside your heart for a new approach, a new possibility. Essentially the "jury is out" on your experiment and all you have to do is withhold judgment to create the space for it to succeed.

Your Sovereign Soul knows exactly what she is doing. There is a rightness to both the challenges and the support that will become part of your daily existence as you become more and more aligned with her. Trust is a huge part of the process. You are trusting her to guide you, and trusting yourself to hear, understand and follow that guidance.

Surrender

The last and most fulfilling aspect of becoming willing is surrender. Just let go. Take your hands off the wheel. This may challenge an independent seeker like you since abdicating authority may be a completely foreign idea for you. But the work that you've done so far has prepared you, and you are ready to step into the liberation of surrender.

Surrendering won't happen for you all at once. You will surrender one thing, and then wrestle control of it back again, just out of habit. You will put it down, only to pick it back up again, almost without knowing what you are doing. The thing that you are actually surrendering is control, and control is hard to let go of when you've been working so hard to hold on to it for so long. But surrender is a profoundly sweet state of mind. In the end, it is all we have ever wanted.

We have wanted to be able to trust life and to feel safe and free, but we have been afraid to do so. The situations and people that we have attempted to surrender to in the past may have betrayed us, either by accident or on purpose. Know that your Sovereign Soul will never betray you. She is the wisest, most holy part of your being and you can completely trust her. All you need to do right now is to allow yourself to surrender. You do the letting go. She will do the catching. Practice. You will become used to the feeling, and you will find the sweetness in it. Just practice and keep on practicing.

Open to the Vision

When you are ready, the next step is for you to open to your own unique vision of a Soul-centered life. This vision will not come solely from you, but will be a beautiful collaboration between you and your Sovereign Soul, as she reveals to you the elements of your authentic expression of that life. You will partner with your Soul, co-creating the journey by actively crafting the vision. When you allow yourself to open to the possibilities, when you ask the right questions, then you will find that the answers surface effortlessly, as though on their own. Your partnership in the process will feel joyful and fulfilling as you do it, and the sudden rush of freedom that comes with abandoning your previously held limitations will further commit you to your own unique expression of Soul.

Your vision will hold all the information that you need about living a Soul-centered life, tailor-made for you. You will describe your lifestyle, your living space, your spiritual practice, your relationship to the Divine and to the world around you, your right livelihood, and your service to life itself. You will know how living a Soul-centered life looks and feels. As you get more and more clear in your vision, you'll know you are on the right track when you feel a surge of energy; a rightness, or an irresistible pull in a certain direction. The more you work with it, the more immediately recognizable that sensation will become to you, and you will learn to follow the pull, exploring the possibilities with confidence. In the beginning, just keep an eye out for that sensation, and when you find it, follow its lead above anything else. Do not let your mind talk you out of your vision, or discourage you, but practice trusting that surge of energy and enthusiasm. Recognize it for what it is; a communication from your Sovereign Soul indicating that you are headed in the right direction.

Visioning Questions

Initially you will want to begin by writing out your vision to get to the heart of it. You may want to start by journaling on the questions I've listed below. These questions are designed to stimulate your sense of possibility and to encourage you to connect with your beautiful Sovereign Soul.

Do not be fooled by the simplicity of the questions. Know that they are only the key to a door. They are neither the door nor what lies behind it. Instead, just take the key in hand and proceed to boldly unlock and open the door, revealing the treasures it holds in store. Release both your skepticism and your expectation and simply be the one who holds the key and is willing to use it. Show up and open the door. Let the questions guide the direction of your thoughts, and let them inspire yet more questions as you go.

This list is by no means comprehensive, nor does it seek to be. It is simply tinder for the bonfire that is your Sovereign Soul's divine expression. Please use accordingly:

ભ If I were to completely commit to a Soul-centered life – what three things about my life would change the most?

ભ How would I present myself differently to the world, if I were truly living a Soul-centered Life?

ભ What would be most important to me?

ભ How would I feel about God?

ભ How would I feel about my Soul?

ભ What would be my greatest blessing to the world?

ભ What would a typical day in my Soul-centered life look like?

ભ If I were to ask my Sovereign Soul what the most important thing is that I can do today to bring myself more into alignment with her, what would she say?

Take your time with these questions. Maybe journal on one or two a day for several weeks. You are fleshing out a blueprint for your identity and your life as a Soul-centered woman, and it is supposed to take a little time. Go back and revisit questions you answered earlier, and answer them again. Leave enough space around your answers so you can fill in insights and flashes of inspiration as they happen. Add questions of your own, if there are areas that these questions did not address that feel important to you. Ask for help all the way through the process – perhaps starting your journaling session with a prayer or meditation. Really open yourself to Divine inspiration, as you work through these ideas.

Other Visioning Techniques

Once you've made a good start at writing out your vision, you can incorporate meditation, visual arts/collage and dream work into your process for further clarification.

You may find it useful to combine these techniques as you expand your visioning process. So you might begin your evening rest by reading your written visioning exercise, leading into a short meditation on it, and then falling asleep with the images and ideas that came up fresh in your mind. When you wake up in the morning you could record your dreams and later that day use images and ideas from your dreams to explore with collage. In this way you can compound the impact of and create momentum around those ideas.

You can find more in-depth information on meditation, art and dream work in the chapter on Building a Spiritual Practice and there are additional visioning resources available in the Sovereign Soul Sanctuary online community at www.sovereignsoul.org.

Establish Themes

The visioning process is a powerful way to create momentum, and also assists you to identify a theme or themes to your journey as you go. In the busy and astoundingly distracting modern world, identifying a theme can create intense focus and movement.

Humans are almost compelled to identify and establish the directional forces at work in our lives. Our very survival has rested upon our ability to do exactly that. Our adaptability as a species is an outcropping of that skill which has so amply contributed to the success of our species so far. We seek out meaning and direction in everything that we do. The only difference is whether we are doing it consciously or subconsciously. We never stop. This is a steady, reliable human tendency. As you begin to work consciously with it, you will learn that you can trust it. It has always served you, and it will serve you now, once you become aware of it, and then work with it to support your focus and momentum.

When used unconsciously, it is usually used to scan new environments for indications of how best be accepted by others – how to be and stay safe. But you can abandon that agenda, and instead begin to scan your life for indications of your Sovereign Soul's guidance. You are looking for clues, for the current trend of energy. You are looking for the theme.

Your Sovereign Soul can indicate themes in a variety of ways. Synchronicity is a particularly potent set of clues, so pay attention. Record coincidences and synchronicities and use them in your journaling and visioning work. Look for clues in the opportunities that surround you, in the correlation between your dreams and your daily life, and in the images and symbols that continue to come up in your explorations.

You are on what is often called the "Hero's Journey" and you will find different stages or themes to that journey as you move through it. Being able to identify and then consciously participate in your current theme will focus and encourage you every step of the way. All you have to do is allow your theme to be revealed to you and then do your best to participate as fully in it as you can. Know also that themes come and go, so be aware when one is closing out and another one is opening up. Your increased awareness and participation will strengthen the flow of communications between you and your Sovereign Soul, and alleviate any impulses that you might have to block that connection. Remember, you are in the process of becoming willing.

A last note on themes, and thematic exploration: Themes are ever present and they are powerful allies when you become conscious of them and agree to participate, but they do not create a simple "paint-by-numbers" situation for you no matter how they are approached. As anyone who has experienced deep loss or grief can tell you, although there are clearly identifiable stages to grieving, and knowing them is helpful, it does not alleviate your need to grieve. As they say, "The map is not the territory." This is really important for you to understand from the beginning.

Mapping Your Journey

Your journal and artwork will describe a map of your journey, but you will only be given bits of the map at a time, and sometimes the map will change in your hands. It is useful, as you compare your map (your understanding of the thematic nature of your current endeavors) to your territory (what you are actually experiencing, both internally and externally at any particular point in time) to know when they align and when they don't and to note any discrepancies between the two.

Themes will profoundly enrich your experience of your journey and provide focal points and structure to your map, but they cannot create an artificial sense of safety or routine for you. To navigate your journey effectively, use themes as loose guidelines and allow a certain amount of flexibility. With that flexibility, you will be able to stay alert to the themes as they shift, but you will not find the need to "marry" any one theme. Themes change, themes expand themselves, and events that meant one thing at one time can mean something completely different at another time.

In working on your map with themes, you will be interpreting your life as you would interpret a dream. Make the assumption that everything has meaning, but never assume that you know what that meaning is. A quest is most identifiable by the questions that attend it, and working with themes simply enriches the *quality of the questions* that you are able to ask at any point in time.

A Few Words of Encouragement

In case you are feeling as though the entire effort is so esoteric and unwieldy that it can neither be neither fathomed nor even embarked upon, know this: Your Sovereign Soul holds the vision for you and that vision is clear and powerful and absolutely right for you and right for the world.

You are not responsible to create the vision for your Sovereign Soul, nor are you capable of blocking the manifestation of that vision. There are things that you can do to support it and there are things you can do to stall it, at least as much as you are able, but you are not the sole author of your purpose here. Thinking that you hold ultimate responsibility for whether it happens or not is simply a case of mistaken identity. It is your Soul who is Sovereign – who stands connected to the Divine Source of All Things and also to your personal experience of your life. It is your Soul that fuels your changes, protects you from unnecessary hardship and is in charge of your lessons and your experiences. You are a participant, willing or otherwise, but you are not driving the bus. Your willingness to surrender to the Divinity within you, your Sovereign Soul, will determine how successfully you are able to navigate the experience of your life.

It may also be helpful for you to remember that this journey is a simple, natural thing for you to do. It is neither mighty, nor mundane. The mystics have long promised us that what we seek also seeks us, and they are right. You are not required to come up with the "right" answers to the questions. You are only required to contemplate and explore them. The rest will be attended to by the Divinity within you that waits, poised and ready, to sail through the clear channel of your willingness.

You are both the vessel and the crew, but the captain is your Sovereign Soul, and she can be trusted. Relax into the knowledge of this and simply perform the tasks before you. Ask the questions. Listen to the answers. Be willing to participate. Cultivate patience and compassion for yourself and your process. You are right where you need to be and you are exactly on time.

Chapter Two
Making Room for Your Sovereign Soul

Now that we've cleared some interior space for your Soul with willingness and surrender, it is time to look at the world around you. The next step in your journey is for you to create space in your physical environments to welcome your Sovereign Soul. You are going to invite her into all the spaces where you routinely spend time, deepening the impact of her presence in your life by echoing it in a tangible, physical way.

What It's Like Now

It may be true that your home does not currently reflect your Sovereign Soul's presence in any way. The mere suggestion that you turn your attention to your physical surroundings may even be creating some anxiety for you. This is to be expected. Your physical environments usually reflect either the needs of your current lifestyle or the state of your inner landscape - usually a combination of both.

If your lifestyle has not supported expression of your Soul, and if that lack of support has resulted in either emotional distress or disconnection, then you can expect your physical environment to be pretty much the opposite of what it would be, if it were to support and fully express your Sovereign Soul. Take heart. Even if you have tried unsuccessfully before to make changes in your physical surroundings, this is a whole new ballgame.

A Whole New Ballgame

There are a couple of powerful and compelling reasons why everything is different now. The first is that you are inviting the assistance of the most powerful part of yourself to initiate and maintain the shifts. This is the part of you that has moved you from painful situations into healthier situations over and over in your life. This is the part of you that has relieved you of inappropriate jobs, unfulfilling relationships, painful habits, and difficult situations. If you have ever in your life been moved from a bad situation to a better one, either by your own actions or by circumstances outside of your control, then you have felt the influence of your Sovereign Soul. So you can trust her.

In the past, a lot of the changes probably happened without your consciously willing them to happen, or even realizing that they needed to happen until they already had. This time you are not only a willing participant, but you are consciously inviting the most powerful part of yourself to enter into the situation and resolve it in a healing way. You are opening your heart and your mind and your life to the Divine influence of your Sovereign Soul and allowing that influence to direct the changes that are about to occur.

If you believe that there are any dark and cluttered corners that your Sovereign Soul can't clear, any loose ends that she can't tie up, then you are mistaken. You don't have to completely believe it yet, but you do have to allow for the *possibility*. You have to allow for the possibility that you may have a mighty partner right there beside you, inspiring you, moving you forward, blowing through your life like a fresh and healthy breeze, clearing what needs clearing and healing what needs healing. You do not have to be afraid.

The second compelling reason that this time will be a different experience for you is that you will be making these changes from within. Instead of muscling through the action part, you are doing the inner work first. This time, you are letting the deepest, highest part of who you are *inspire* the exact shifts that you are going to make. When they are inspired from within, rather than forced upon you from without, those shifts will feel delicious. And delicious has momentum.

The Big Delicious Difference

Have you ever felt inspired to do a small decorative thing and spontaneously done it with whatever you happen to have handy? And after you did it, didn't you feel a sense of comfort and satisfaction every time you saw it? Didn't you wonder why you hadn't done it a long time ago? Weren't you amazed by what a Big Delicious Difference a tiny little change could make? That's what Divinely-inspired changes to your physical space will feel like. That *exact* feeling is what you are after. That's the target. That is the feeling of satisfying your Sovereign Soul and it is enough to combat any level of previously held inertia or overwhelm.

Space Matters

So let's start by looking at physical space itself. The physical realm has an extremely powerful influence on you. It starts with your physical body, extends out into the rooms in your home, the environment surrounding your home, the methods of transportation you use to move your physical body from one environment to the next, all the various environments in which you spend the bulk of your time, and, on a larger scale, the natural world around you and even further still, the earth, the universe and beyond.

In most cases, it can be difficult for even the most inspired ideas, loving feelings, or beautiful dreams to survive in environments that present perpetual disturbances. That's why we started first by creating space in your heart and mind before we attempted to create space in the physical world. You will discover that once you have some space in your interior, it is easier to make it happen on the exterior. Your Sovereign Soul will need to inspire and support the changes you are about to make in your physical world, so it is useful to have opened the connection to her a little before attempting to shift the physical world. Your physical world may at times overpower the best intentions of your personality but they cannot impede your Soul.

Part of the Solution

The powerful impact your physical surroundings have on you is something you can use to your advantage if you use it consciously. Environments can either support you or undermine you. They can enrich your experience of the Divine, or help to create the illusion of separation from the Divine. It's all up to you. When you change your environment, you change your state of mind, and your energetic composition. That's what we are working on now. If your environments have been part of the "problem" before, we are shifting them to become part of the solution.

To begin, the goal is simply to seek out the qualities in your environments that already support your connection to your Sovereign Soul and then echo those qualities wherever possible. Later you will go on to identify areas where physical disturbances are creating the illusion of separation from your Soul, and you'll begin to minimize or eliminate those disturbances. The whole of this exercise will consist of these very basic goals and simple activities all the way through. You'll emphasize what is working for you and clear what is working against you. That's it!

A Warm Welcome

Before you start, you may find it helpful to create a powerful mindset for this activity. This is not about faulting yourself for clutter, or shaming yourself for dust bunnies. Instead, you can let it be a beautiful celebration. This can be a welcome home, if you allow it to be.

You are in loving service to the most Divine and Holy part of yourself; your beloved Sovereign Soul. And you are preparing the temple for her arrival. Creating a welcoming space for the most precious part of who you are. By engaging in this exercise with devotion, you will indicate that you are willing to allow her fully into your life and to truly live your life with your Soul at the very center of it.

From this perspective, the emotions of overwhelm, shame and blame couldn't be further from your mind. You are not cleaning your house because you are a slob. Instead, you are in loving and devoted service to your Sacred Sovereign Soul. It is your privilege to clear space for her, and add the elements of welcome to that space.

Make your preparations an expression of devotion and love. You have so much to be grateful for that your beautiful Soul has made possible in your life. As you begin, take a moment to count the many ways in which she has supported, protected and delighted you in your life. Think about the ways in which you have been blessed over and over. It may be helpful to actually make a list of them. Once you have allowed yourself to experience that gratitude and devotion, then you can begin the task from that foundation.

Each time you find yourself slipping back into the old-school shame game, stop yourself. Breathe. Remember, you are not a housekeeper - you are a devotee. The work you do here, *any* work that you do here, is holy, and your efforts are blessed by that intention. You are physically demonstrating your love for the highest part of you, your constant inspiration and protector. You are showing your Sovereign Soul how very much you love her with every space you clear for her. Don't let yourself forget that.

Loving the Threshold

Whenever one begins to make a change in the physical world there is a tiny threshold space that shows up. As you prepare yourself to make the change, a tiny moment of balance happens. For a brief moment, the power of your intention is perfectly balanced against the influence of the existing physical space. At this exact moment, it really could go either way. Either you could change the environment with the force of your intention or, upon contemplating the state of the environment, you could be influenced by its inertia, and resign yourself to leaving it as is. Everybody has had this moment. I'll give you an example.

Thinking about your home, you reflect upon a particularly cluttered cupboard. It's an odd-shaped cupboard, too big for small things and too small for big things, so consequentially it has become a catch-all in your home. Most of the items in this particular cupboard are things you haven't seen in months. It's hard to get in and out of there, you don't really know exactly what the contents of the cupboard consist of, but you know that the only reason you'll go into it is to look for something you really, really need and cannot find. The cupboard is a last resort for you.

So you determine that you are going to completely clean out just that one cupboard and you set aside an afternoon to tackle the cupboard. It pleases you to think about how it will look, and how you will feel when you open it up to find it neatly organized, storing useful items in a manner that allows you to find them. Eager to get started, you open the cupboard and then you stand there. You take in the sight for one long moment. This is the moment. The image you had in your head of the purged and neatly organized cupboard is poised, perfectly balanced with the current state of disarray that stands before you. In that moment, the threshold moment, it could go either way.

You might begin to pull items out of the cupboard with a renewed vigor and organize them. Or, just as easily, you might become overwhelmed by the current physical reality of the cupboard, the length of time that it's been like that, and your perceived sensation of the amount of effort it would take to shift the inertia. You might walk away and determine to tackle it another day. That's the threshold moment.

Barrier or Opportunity

The threshold moment represents both a barrier, *and* an opportunity. On the one hand, it's a barrier because it has offered you a chance to turn back, and it has given you incentive to do so. But on the other hand, it is an opportunity because it has also offered you a chance to strengthen your intention, and to press on, thereby strengthening your ability to affect choice and move your vision from your internal world into your physical world.

If this were a video game, this moment would be the moment a super villain appeared and offered you an opportunity to battle. If you've ever played a video game, or watched one being played, you know that if your character is victorious, she comes out of it with powers and tools that she could not have obtained any other way. This moment is exactly like that.

If you are going to be able to fully live into your potential as a spiritual being, your Sovereign Soul will require that you develop the ability to overcome inertia. This skill will be applicable everywhere in your life. You will need the ability to stand in that threshold moment and then, *step over it* instead of turning back. The more threshold moments you are presented with, the more graceful and inevitable that step becomes.

Managing Overwhelm

Another barrier you may experience as you move into the physical realm with your shifts is the sensation of overwhelm. Overwhelm will generally nip your intention in the bud as soon as it senses you even beginning to consider a shift. You can usually encounter it as a string of thoughts accompanied by an ever increasing sensation of anxiety. Overwhelm can literally run you off the road before you even get the key in the ignition. It's immediate and massive.

You know the feeling – as if you are being completely bulldozed before you can even form the intention. Stopped cold in your tracks, you turn away from not only the beginnings of your idea, but from anything that even remotely *reminds* you of the idea.

Overwhelm will show up whenever you either try to do something that might dramatically change your circumstances or you attempt to enter into an activity that feels unknown to you. Because it shows up early, before you've had a chance to even form a solid intention or build any energy around that intention, overwhelm is often successful. It can shut you up and shut you down before you even know what hit you. But overwhelm is an illusion. Its strength is purely fictional, and you have to buy into the fiction in order for it to work. Once you recognize it for what it is, you can defeat it - maybe not forever, but at least for the time being. And "for the time being" is all you need.

Recognize the Opponent

Our first resource to manage overwhelm is recognition. When you know what you are dealing with, and what its function is, then you can disconnect it from its power source, which is you. So it may be useful to get really familiar with what Granddaddy Overwhelm feels like when it's in the room.

It may help to actually visualize it, give it a tangible shape. This might sound counter-productive, as though you are giving it power by giving it form, but when you are working with something whose primary strength is the fact that you *don't recognize it consciously,* having the ability to spot it right off can be crucial. Go ahead and let it have a shape, a face, a name. Let it be easily identifiable so that you become immediately aware of its presence and you can clearly see it for what it is.

Understand the Ambush

The next step is to get very clear on how it works. The primary function of an Overwhelm Ambush is to literally stop you before you start. The key here is "*before* you start." The reason this strategy needs to stop you before you start is that its central power lies in your belief that the thing you are about to do cannot be done. But if you were to even start doing it, you would see that it *was* doable. It might not be done perfectly, it might not even be done well, it might not be done the way you wanted to do it, but it was doable.

When you start a thing, you begin to form a feedback loop of information that directly contradicts the central message of Overwhelm, which is that it "can't be done." Because Overwhelm relies completely on your buying into that myth, the second you start to disprove it and do the thing that "could not be done" the myth dissolves in front of you. You may face other barriers and challenges along the way, but the initial ogre of Overwhelm will have been dismantled and dissolved. Understanding this simple truth is key.

Simply Begin

Once you understand that principle, the next step is simply to begin. The bigger the Overwhelm, the tinier your gesture needs to be. You can break the act of beginning down into the smallest increments. You can break it down into a tiny space of time (I will begin this project for exactly 5 minutes, set the timer, and allow myself to stop at 5 minutes if I feel like it!) or a tiny action (I am going to pull the weeds in this one square foot of garden, and then I can be done for the day if I so choose) or a combination of both (I am going to find 10 items in the next five minutes that I can throw out!).

What happens when you give yourself an *incremental task* and *permission to stop when you've finished* is a series of things:

ℛ You break the illusion that the inertia in the environment is more powerful than you are.

ℛ You strengthen your intention by modeling the behavior for yourself.

ℛ You communicate your willingness to act on intention in future.

ℛ And finally, you create that most delicious friend, Momentum.

The Magic of Momentum

Momentum is the natural enemy of Overwhelm. Just as it takes more effort to start something that is not yet in motion, it also takes energy to stop something that is already in motion. So you have only one real objective with your tiny incremental gesture of a task:

You are going to create the *tiniest sliver* of momentum.

And then you are going to observe.

Just observe the power of incremental change, and the addition of even the smallest bit of momentum to a situation that has remained static for any length of time. You will be amazed.

So the exercise goes like this:

ℛ Recognize when you are dealing with Overwhelm,

೫ Understand what it wants and where it is weak,

೫ Apply a teeny tiny bit of momentum (the antidote),

೫ And watch the momentum take over.

This strategy alone will support you in every area of your life, particularly where an internal shift wants to find expression in the physical realm around you.

Sharing Space

As you begin to try to make space for your Soul-centered life, another barrier you might experience is sharing that space with other people. Whether you live alone or with others, your physical surroundings are always impacted by the existence of others who share space with you in some way.

Sometimes the other people in the environments will actively participate in the very inertia you are trying to overcome – they keep the cluttered spaces cluttered, they disregard the qualities that you are cultivating and overlay them with qualities of their own. Even when you are out in the wilderness contemplating an ancient Sequoia, you can still find your meditation interrupted by the presence of noisy hikers or the trash they left behind. Other people are unavoidable and can sometimes frustrate your attempts to work with physical space.

For example, imagine you finally clear off the dining room table, polish the surface and arrange a bowl of water with a few flowers floating in it for a centerpiece. You light some candles and you tell your family that from now on this will be the place where you meet as a family at the end of the day to share a meal and conversation. From now on, you say, this table is not a dumping ground for anything that happens to be in your hands when you walk in the door. They all agree.

The next day you get home from work to find the table strewn with the same old collection of items, the candle knocked over by the cat, and someone has thrown their jacket carelessly over the flower arrangement. Your efforts didn't last 24 hours. Frustrating, yes? Especially now, because now you know how much it warmed your heart to come out into the kitchen earlier that morning and see the table shiny and clean and welcoming. You know how much better your day was when you could sit for a few minutes at the table, light a candle, drink your morning coffee and collect your thoughts. When you were relaxed and peaceful and connected. Those few moments of order and calm had changed your whole day. Now you've come home to find your good work undone and completely overridden by the brute force of other people's habits. How disappointing!

In addition to your disappointment, you may even feel profoundly protective of the shifts that you made. What you are protecting is a pathway to something very precious and sorely missed. The sensation of having recovered even a small bit of the "lost" route to your Sovereign Soul is so essentially comforting and inspiring that it's hard not to leap to its defense.

It may be useful to think of the others in your environment as *part of the environment* and allow their presence, interference and disruption to function much as the previously described threshold moments did - as opportunities to strengthen your commitment.

Think about mowing a lawn or raking up leaves. You fully expect the work to be undone, and you fully expect to be doing it again, just as part of a regular maintenance schedule. Maintenance schedules are much easier to maintain once they're put in place – that's the magic of momentum. It's just that first effort that will take so much energy. Over time, as you fortify the momentum, those who share space with you will begin to become accustomed to having the space cleared, and may perhaps join you in maintaining the space. In the meantime, do your best to see their impact on your physical space as simply a neutral part of the environment, like leaves falling from the tree or grass growing in the lawn. They are just fulfilling their part in the cycle of chaos to order to chaos to order again.

Just as you did with threshold moments, each time you meet a challenge, you strengthen your ability to reconnect with your vision of a Soul-centered life and to respond with intention. As you do, you become more creative and adaptable, but most of all you find out what your bottom line is. You discover what you *need* versus what you merely want. You discover the essential qualities in the things you truly need and you discover ways to bring those qualities into your life. You will know what you are willing to surrender and what you are not. This information may cost you something emotionally but once you've got it, it's yours forever.

Elements of a Soulful Space

There are several key elements that create a welcoming space for your Sovereign Soul. As you read about each one, take a moment to contemplate the quality and the sensation it creates in you. Try to stay out of comparison mode – thinking about whether or not your current environments have these qualities or what it would take to get them. Right now, all we want to do is get a feel for them. If you can stay out of judging yourself or blaming yourself, this will be a very pleasurable exercise. Later we can address practical steps for making any changes you want to make, and dealing with any barriers that may come up. For now just suspend your judgment and enjoy the *sensation* of the qualities as you read through them.

Spaciousness

Spaciousness is the most basic inviting quality that welcomes your Sovereign Soul into your life. It doesn't necessarily have to be a literal expanse of physical space in your environment - it could just be the *feeling* of being able to relax, stretch out, move about, to fully breathe.

Clutter is not welcoming at all to your Soul. It cannot inspire expansive ideas and soulful activities. So the simple act of removing clutter and crowding can make a very small space feel spacious. A spacious environment will not have a lot of items, and will have no redundancy among the items it does contain. For example, a beautifully painted wall with a single, striking piece of art has a profoundly more spacious feeling than a similarly sized wall with several competing or contrasting pieces of art. Even though both walls may be about the same size, and the collection of art on the second wall does not actually take up more space in the room than the single piece of art on the first wall, the more sparsely decorated wall will create a sensation of spaciousness that the "busy" wall cannot.

People who feel a lack in one area of their lives may tend to collect things in other areas. So if you feel pressed for time, or feel your financial situation does not fully support you, or that the space you live in is smaller than you would like it to be – you may tend to accumulate clutter in response. The sensation of not having enough can make you want to hold onto whatever you have, resulting in either "too much of a good thing" or the frustration of endless possibilities.

You may recognize this in your art drawer, or your fabric drawer, or your closet or your garage. These are all places where the things you "just might need someday…" usually come to rest - graveyards for the skeletons of all the things you *meant* to do but never quite got around to doing. You've probably held these items in your hands from time to time and tried to decide whether you should get rid of them, but then decided not to. You wanted the option to use them "someday" in the nebulous future, so you put them back in the drawer, or the closet or the garage, and promptly forgot about them.

It is important to recognize that what drove that choice was a feeling that there isn't enough in the world and if you were to let go of this one thing you might not find another one. Or you might get another one but it wouldn't be as good as this one and you would be stuck with something crappy so you better hang on to this one for dear life! That exact feeling and the set of beliefs that accompany it all combine to function as a block to the open flow of communication with your Sovereign Soul.

Instead, when you choose to surrender items that you no longer need or aren't yet ready to use, you commit a profound act of trust. The decision removes you from the hoarding mentality and makes you a contributor in the world, part of *the flow* of physical reserves. The hoarding mentality is a supremely effective illusion which traps you in the mistaken belief that you are somehow separated from your Sovereign Soul and from Source itself.

Every time you cram your physical space full of things you do not use or need, you actively crowd out your Sovereign Soul. You create a situation where you literally have no space to welcome her, and you tell yourself and your Soul that she cannot be trusted to provide for you. This key concept is so important that if you stopped reading right here - if you put the book down and began to identify and eliminate all hoarding beliefs and behaviors in your life - you will have won a major victory. Just this one shift can dramatically change your spiritual life and your experience of yourself as a spiritual being. It is impossible for me to overstate this.

Let's contemplate spaciousness, then. You have achieved a state of spaciousness when:

Your surroundings contain blank areas – airy, empty, or light spaces.

You have clear empty spaces on counters, tables, shelves and surfaces.

You have only one of each of the things that you need, and it is the right one for the space and for the purpose.

You feel like your physical space is only about forty to fifty percent "full."

You have room for more - in your drawers, your closets, your bookshelves and file cabinets.

Take a moment now and just imagine what that would feel like. Picture opening up your file cabinet and having room for about 30% more files, if you wanted to. No jamming and squeezing to add a new file or paperwork to an old file. The hanging files actually swayed when you pulled the drawer out. Delicious, yes?

Now imagine that your clothes closet is equally spacious. You pull open the closet door and you can easily slide the hangers back and forth. If you have shelves, there are spaces in between the stacks of sweaters, and none of the stacks come even close to reaching the top of the space. When you open your drawers, there is plenty of room to add an item from the laundry, and that item is easily located the next day.

Now imagine yourself looking around at the surfaces in your house. Your bedside table is clear of all items that are not absolutely essential. Your dining room table is bare, except maybe for a nice centerpiece and some placemats. It is waiting there for the family to gather around for dinner. When you sit at the table during the day, there is space to relax, to chat with a guest, to read a magazine, whatever you would like to do. All throughout your home there is plenty of space. Isn't this is a lavish feeling. Isn't this luxurious? You wouldn't think it, but the feeling of luxury is *less* stuff, not *more* stuff! This is the sensation that a welcoming space creates, for you, and for your Sovereign Soul.

Things are like thoughts. When you are surrounded and crowded by stuff, it's like having your mind chattering at you all the time. When your mind and your physical spaces are "chattering" constantly, it's hard to hear the still, quiet voice of your Sovereign Soul.

Clearing the space around you allows you to better sense the presence of your beautiful Soul. And once you begin to sense her presence, once you start to fall in love with the sound of her voice instead of the chatter of your stuff, I promise you will never miss a single thing that you had to surrender for it to come forth!

Body Spaciousness

Another kind of spaciousness that you might want to consider is body spaciousness. Allowing your body to experience spaciousness is profoundly healing, not just physically but emotionally and mentally as well.

Body spaciousness is all about purification. The three basic ways to work with purification (fasting, breath work, and detoxification) are covered later in the chapter on Building a

Spiritual Practice. It should be noted that before working with any of them you should consult with your physician and to take into account your current state of health. Each of these three methods of creating spaciousness in your physical body can have profound and possibly unexpected effects on you, so it is best to approach them in moderation and with careful consideration just to be safe.

Most of all I want to continue to remind you that your body is yet another physical environment *in which you find yourself*, and each of the qualities discussed in this chapter can be applied to the body (as an environment) as well as to the larger environments that surround you.

Movement

The next quality that invites a Soul-centered life is movement. Physical environments that allow for the flow of energy are wonderfully welcoming to your Sovereign Soul. You may not have thought of it consciously before, but on some level you can probably feel when a space allows energy to move and when it doesn't.

Stagnation

Stagnation (the opposite of movement) is extremely uncomfortable, both physically and energetically. It's also very obvious, even if you only register it as a feeling of being trapped, sluggish, or even just wanting to leave that space in a hurry. You might not know *why* you feel it, but you definitely feel it.

Consider whether you have some spaces that create the sensation in you. They will probably be spaces that have been abandoned and filled with all kinds of clutter and debris. They could be limited to specific corners or sections of your house. The trunk of your car could be a stagnant space. Even a single piece of furniture can create the sensation – like the chair that nobody ever sits in to read a book, the loveseat that people use to pile their belongings on, the wardrobe that is jammed full and never opened, for example.

Targeting Stagnation

A very powerful way to get energy moving in a room is to target and eliminate dust, pet hair, or any mildew in the space. These things will collect where stagnation persists, so they can be a great alert system for you. If you've been living in stagnant environments for a while, you may not at first notice dust building up on things. You may have trained yourself to ignore the pet fur, or the slight smell of mildew in a single corner of the house, for example.

Once you allow yourself to become sensitized to it, it will be easy to shift your weekly routine to target those areas. You will be amazed at how simply clearing the byproducts of stagnation can eliminate the sensation of stagnation completely. Those areas will probably always have a *predisposition* toward stagnation, so they will always need your attention, but the maintenance will be much easier than the initial elimination effort.

Move Your Body

The environment of your physical body can also support your Soul-centered life when you apply the principle of movement to it. There are many ways you can include soulful movement in your life without beginning a serious exercise regime. If you already do a lot of movement, but you do it in a distracted or goal-oriented way, you will find a difference in both quality and results when you experiment with *soulful* movement. We will explore soulful movement in more depth in a later chapter, but for now it is enough to recognize that movement in your body can become a way to welcome your Sovereign Soul if you let it.

Any part of your body that does not experience movement on a regular basis will begin to collect stagnant energy. Any movement you can offer your body and bless with your awareness becomes a clearing point for that stagnant energy, cleaning and refreshing it. Keep in mind, that your body is a profoundly powerful environment in which small shifts can create massive change, so please consult with your physician if you have any health concerns about movement, or before embarking upon any new movement-related routine!

Natural Elements

In addition to spaciousness and movement, your Sovereign Soul is particularly receptive to the natural elements in your environments. Being in nature, surrounded by the elements and other living things, invigorates every aspect of your life, but it is particularly stimulating to your spiritual aspects.

The natural world demonstrates the cycles and balance that we crave. It models systems that work and it does so in a way that we can internalize immediately, even below the level of our conscious awareness. Nature is powerful medicine. Two ways to tap into that power are first to get out into natural environments as often as possible, and second to find ways to bring the natural world into your regular environments so that you never feel disconnected from it.

Most of us don't spend enough time in natural settings, and the quality of time that we spend there when we do is usually compromised by the activities we've chosen or the company we keep while we're there. Of course, any time spent in nature can be healing and strengthening to your connection with the Divine - even if the only time you spend in nature includes distracting activities and company, it is still worth doing and will benefit you.

However, you may find it useful to introduce a few undistracted opportunities simply for the experience and to discover an even more beneficial result. Remember, absolutes and extremes are not required for you to connect with your Sovereign Soul. Just continue to refine what you are already doing, bringing greater and greater awareness to it as you do.

Fresh Air

Fresh air can bring both movement and purification to the energy of a space. If your environment is climate-controlled with windows that don't open, or no windows at all, simply moving the air with a small fan can help. Of course, the best solution would be to have windows you can open and keeping them open whenever possible.

Natural Light

Sunlight is another powerful natural element that creates movement and purification in a physical space. Changing either the quality or the quantity of light in a room can completely change the energy of the room and your physical response to it. Natural sunlight is the most refreshing light to shift energy in a room. Introduce as much natural sunlight into the space as you can to rid a room of stagnation. If natural sunlight is not available, there are other options that can clear the energy and create a welcome for your Sovereign Soul.

Full spectrum lighting choices are available almost everywhere. You can also change lighting fixtures so that they provide warm, clean, diffused light in pleasant colors (via lampshades, colored bulbs, etc.) that lift the energy of the room and create a calm, open feeling. As you work with light, try to notice corners and areas that get no light at all and do your best to eliminate as many of them as possible. You may even want to rearrange the furniture to better "enlighten" the room if you have to. Experiment with it and see how you feel.

Don't forget to let your body get some light. We all know the dangers of exposure to the sun, but when well protected, the body loves a little natural light. Try to let your body out into the sun (with full protection of course) whenever possible.

Living Plants

Even if you have no green thumb, the presence of living plants in your home, your office and all the spaces you inhabit regularly will shift your relationship to those spaces and to yourself within them. Plants demand certain conditions that may not be obvious to you at first. They require certain amounts of light, water, air quality, and other naturally beneficial conditions regularly, so they can act as a sort of barometer for you. Even if you've not noticed a lack of light, or a point of stagnation in your home, your plants will point it out to you.

Plants also keep you on a balanced schedule. Those of us who do not naturally have a green thumb are usually people who are in some way disconnected from a balanced, rhythmic way of life. We move in fits and starts. We feast or fall to famine. We abstain, and then over-indulge. None of these tendencies work well for plants, and even the hardiest and most forgiving plant will eventually make the limitations of such habits extremely obvious.

If you are a person who believes you cannot be trusted with a plant, then you are exactly the person who may find the most benefit in having even one. The plant will support your intentions to live a more centered and sustainable lifestyle, and, in doing so, add an element of natural healing energy to your physical surroundings.

Water Elements

The element of water is also a profoundly beneficial addition to your environment if you seek to deeply connect with the most soulful part of who you are. Metaphorically speaking, water represents purification and the Soul itself, both of which speak directly to the parts of you that have been waiting a long time for expression.

Any possible way that you can introduce the element of water to your home, inside or out, will clear and heal and inspire you. An indoor fountain is always a good choice, as are things like fishbowls and aquariums. Fishbowls and aquariums have the added benefit of introducing living creatures to your surroundings which amplify the positive effect of the natural element and create balanced, rhythmic habits, much as plants do. Keeping your fish happy and thriving is a great way to cultivate a sense of healing routine and purification in your life. It takes attention, consistency and compassion to have healthy, happy fish, just as it does to have a healthy, happy relationship with your Sovereign Soul.

As always, your body remains another powerful environment in which to make these qualitative shifts. One way to introduce the water element into your physical surroundings is to literally soak your body in it. Healing baths and showers are profoundly uplifting to your Spirit when done with the appropriate attention and intention. Pay attention to purity of the water with a filter, and use aromatic salts, oils and minerals to enhance the healing potential of the bath.

Your physical body is the single most constant and intimate environment you experience every day. Let your body sink into the healing waters on a regular basis, and keep your bathroom clear of stagnation and clutter of any kind. This is one room where the water element can most support you spiritually, and it deserves particular attention on a regular basis as you prepare your body-temple to commune with and receive your Sovereign Soul.

In other rooms of the house, it may be useful to keep glass containers of purified water and a clean, pretty glass readily available. This will introduce the element of water to the room and will remind you how much your physical being loves and needs water. You can create an element of ritual around keeping the container full, polishing it until it shines, placing it in a space where it gets natural light during the day, and taking the time to drink it with intention and attention.

By letting water take a sacred place in your home and thereby engaging with it, you create a powerful reminder of your willingness to let what is soulful take a prominent role in your life. Every time you participate in this ritual, you send a message of willingness to your Sovereign Soul. You can think of it as an elemental act.

Fire Elements

Fire is another element that can powerfully change the energy of a room. Candles and incense can be useful, but be sure that you approach them with a light touch, since many people can become overwhelmed by the smell of scented candles and incense. You want to start with fragrance-free candles at first, and if you do decide to use some sort of incense start with something subtle such as lemongrass, or sweet grass. Avoid starting out with anything heavy or lingering as you do not want to create an unpleasant sensation. Imagine you are preparing for the arrival of a beloved guest, and do not choose anything that might be off-putting to them. Instead you want to create a warm, subtle, welcoming sensation in your heart, and in your home.

Be sensitive to any allergies you may or may not know you have, and pay close attention to your physical responses to any shifts that you've made. Your body is your best advisor. Adding a natural scent to your home is hardly useful if your body receives it as a disruption. If you have known allergies and asthma, consult with your physician first to ensure any changes you make to the air quality in your home will align with your other health goals.

If you do not want to add candles or incense, there are other ways to stimulate the feeling of fire – there are some wonderful fake fireplaces that have a very realistic effect, there are candles that are battery operated but appear to flicker, and there are lovely natural salt lamps that release negative ions into the atmosphere of a room and give a warm rosy glow to the space. All of these additions can add the element of fire without some of the considerations and cautions that actual fire can introduce. Please be mindful of all safety considerations when working with the element of fire in your physical spaces. If you do decide to add actual fire, incense or candles, as always be cautious in handling them, and never leave them unattended. Fire is a powerful, stimulating and purifying element, but it should be handled with due respect.

Adding the element of fire to your body is usually best done with warmth itself – you can work with heated rice pillows on pressure points or over specific areas of the body that need movement and purification (joints, lymph nodes, kidneys, etc.). Food and beverages can also be warming, particularly when they involve the warming spices. The Ayurvedic tradition is rich with information on bringing the element of fire to the body through certain foods and spices, so that may be something you choose to explore. You may also want to explore different types of saunas and steam rooms, or hot rock massage to bring the element of fire to your body. As always, consult with your physician beforehand to ensure that your choices align with your other health goals.

Other Natural Elements

In addition to fresh air, sunlight, living things, water and fire, there are many other natural elements that you can add to connect your physical spaces with nature. Many people find that rocks, stones, minerals and shells can create a calming, grounding energy in a room that previously felt sterile or devoid of energy. Wood can also be a healing element to add; pieces of wood, wood sculptures or wood furniture can be very effective. Wearing jewelry made of natural elements or carrying stones, shells and feathers on your person can add the influence of these natural elements to the environment of your body.

You may want to introduce the elements of nature into your physical space by adding pictures of natural settings. You can change the pictures to accompany the seasons, (which is also wonderful for creating that sensation of movement in a room), or you can choose your pictures based solely upon the elements you want to introduce. A photograph of a sunset can bring more fire into the room, or you can choose a waterfall for water, or a mountain for earth, or birds flying across a beautiful sky for air. Pictures of animals in natural settings are another way to bring the energy of living things into your space. Any picture that creates a sensation of calm spaciousness in you will be a wonderful addition.

Remember that you are speaking to your Sovereign Soul through your five senses, and you are allowing the feelings that these shifts create in you to become feedback from her. As you experiment with these small changes you begin to feel a resonance with your Soul. The connection has moved out of your mind, and you engage with her through your body itself. You are beginning to recognize your Sovereign Soul by the feel of her.

You will probably also notice yourself becoming increasingly sensitive to environments that don't resonate with your Sovereign Soul. You may walk into a space where you've been many times before and suddenly it will feel oppressive and stagnant or sterile, like something is missing. You have always been impacted by your environments, but your newly heightened awareness now allows you to notice the impact and you can engage or disengage with it from a position of *choice*. This offers you the opportunity to create yet another channel through which you can experience resonance with your Sovereign Soul.

The Power of Beauty

All forms of beauty have great power to inspire you and strengthen your connection to the Divine. What you find most beautiful appeals to you because it reminds you of your Sovereign Soul and offers an opportunity to connect with her more fully. When you find something truly beautiful, every part of you responds to it. The more you can surround yourself with that kind of beauty, the more frequently and profoundly you will experience the Divine every day.

This is the way your Sovereign Soul speaks to you most often and most recognizably. Whatever you consider most beautiful will affect you most immediately and is what you most need in order to feel the presence of the Divine in your life. It creates the state of mind that best allows you to open yourself of that presence.

Introducing beauty to your physical environments and emphasizing the beauty that already exists there will be a pleasurable and fulfilling activity for you. In addition to stimulating your centers of joy, it will ignite your creative spirit. You will be working with textures, flavors, colors, sounds, scents and images that delight your senses. The wide world will open up and become a treasure hunt, with you hot on the trail for that which delights you and fills you up on every level. When you see these things, or hear them, or touch them, all points within you will wake up, open up and rejoice. Sometimes very beautiful things can stimulate deep emotions other than joy. Collect and surround yourself with whatever it is that can move you deeply just by its presence.

Keeping Beauty Fresh

Remember that even great beauty can lose its impact on you over time, as you become accustomed to it and eventually unaware of it. Pay attention to how the beauty you have collected around you is impacting you. Once an item no longer creates a soulful state of mind in you, remove it and replace it with one more potently beautiful. The idea is to keep beauty fresh and expressive of your current tastes and themes. You are strengthening the communication with your Sovereign Soul by letting her to tell you from day to day what most supports and revitalizes your bond with her.

We need different things at different times, and the music that most perfectly fills us with inspired joy one day may not have the same impact on a different day. Respect for that reality can give you access to greater possibilities. When you are inspired to let things come and go as they move you, you emphasize your willingness to seek and maintain *only that which is appropriate to you in that moment*. You are learning not to cling to things out of habit, a sense of lack or limitation. This is a very powerful lesson that will serve you well.

If you need stimulation to create that awareness, let the changing of the months, personal holidays throughout the year, changing seasons, or some other marker be your guide. Create a structure that will support your process, as long as it doesn't limit your options and become a routine. If you can combine structure with flexibility then you are truly available to your Soul's directive.

Structure and Beauty

Structure is a wonderful tool to create new habits and awareness. It can function as a gentle reinforcement of the positive choices we've made, and as a remedy for inertia. However, if you find yourself always doing the exact same thing every time the reinforcement arrives, you limit the possibility of being of open to your Soul's direction. So you want to use the structure to trigger a question, rather than letting it be an answer.

For example, if one of your triggers is a holiday season, but every time that holiday arrives you pull out the same decorations and arrange them in exactly the same way, because that is your tradition, then you limit the ability of your Soul to speak to you through that particular manifestation of beauty.

Instead, ask for guidance, and allow what is appropriate at this exact time and space to bubble to the surface. Your Sovereign Soul will surprise you. Sometimes she will crave the familiar beauty of your traditional arrangement, and other times she will ask for something completely different. Following that guidance will allow you to truly benefit from the full impact beauty can have on your spiritual life and on your deepening love for your Sovereign Soul.

Your Beautiful Body

As always, I'd like bring the element of beauty to the body. Many of us are not accustomed to exploring, perceiving or receiving the blessing of the beauty of our own bodies. We apply externally dictated standards of beauty to the environment of our body more so than with any other environment we inhabit.

Most of us, no matter how trendy something is, interior design-wise, would not consider rearranging our homes to match it if it didn't already resonate with us on some level anyway. It's a strange thing. If we thought it was ugly, we would probably not redecorate our home in that manner no matter how hip the design was. We might dress for trends, but we rarely decorate for trends. This is probably because we see the home as being something we have to live in every day, rather than just for a brief span.

The reality is that we live in our bodies even more permanently and intimately than we do our homes, yet many of us think nothing of letting the world tell us what is and isn't beautiful about our bodies. Then we try to apply the standards of beauty enforced by the world at large. Add that to the societal bias against self-appreciation or any form of expression that could remotely resemble "vanity" and you have a perfect recipe for failing to recognize or appreciate the beauty of your own body.

To start, it is enough to work with your individual sense of beauty in the larger surrounding environments, and simply to devote a few moments a day to admiring or creating small bits of beauty in your physical body. Allow yourself to admire your skin, if that's what's beautiful to you right now, and don't let your weight or your wrinkles or your split ends or your stretch marks (or whatever other part of you that you don't love yet) overshadow it.

Experiment a little with color in your wardrobe; add some jewelry, trying a hairstyle - just *play* with the concept of perceiving beauty in, on or around your body, rather than embarking upon some radical self improvement program. The goal is to simply create a habit of *noticing and letting yourself receive* the beauty that *already exists* in your body right now and then strengthening that sensation by allowing yourself to honor that beauty with your full attention! The process is the point, and it should be pleasurable. You add experiences of beauty in your body the same way you add elements of beauty in your other environments – gradually and with great appreciation. We're not fixing you. We're <u>*loving*</u> you.

Now that you've made room for your Sovereign Soul in your physical environments, you'll want to make time for her in your life. You'll approach it in much the same way you did physical space – gradual movement, small shifts and a gentle expansion in the direction of your Soul-centered life. So let's get started!

Chapter Three
Making Time for Your Sovereign Soul

Like every relationship, your relationship with your Sovereign Soul will need time enough to develop and strengthen. If you are truly committed to living a Soul-centered life, you'll need to begin to prioritize your relationship with your Soul above all other things, and that can be easier said than done. Let's face it, time is the one thing we never seem to have enough of and the lack of it is the first thing we point to when we describe our inability to make a change. But your ability to work with this challenge may be the most powerful thing you can do for yourself and for your relationship with your Sovereign Soul.

A lot of the difficulty spiritual seekers experience when they try to create time for their spiritual practice is the belief that it can't be just any random sort of time. It must be a certain quality of time to be considered spiritual. It can't be busy, hurried time. It has to be enough time to allow you to settle into something. Time to settle down and shake off the frenzy of your day at least long enough to let the more subtle shifts occur.

So we think we can't just cram spiritual pursuits into the day wherever we find a spare moment and we might be at least a little bit right about that. It is true that the quality of the time that you devote to spiritual pursuits will affect the quality of the pursuit itself. But it is *not* true that if you don't have a long, quiet, uninterrupted stretch of devotional time, you shouldn't attempt to connect with the Divine at all.

The "Perfect Moment"

The creative impulse is very close to the spiritual impulse and artists and writers often make the same mistake spiritual seekers do – they wait for the "Perfect Creative Moment" to happen before they will begin. The belief is that if a moment cannot offer everything, it cannot offer anything and that is simply not true. Spirit doesn't work like that. Your Sovereign Soul can and does work with any and every moment that you offer to her. She can use it all.

The important lesson for both the creative person and the spiritual seeker is the same: Come as you are. Both art and faith require that you come exactly as you are, without perfection, without your idealized version of how it should look and feel. You are asked to *just show up*. For a spiritual person, this means cultivating devotional *momentum* by allowing shorter, perhaps less "ideal" moments carry your spiritual intentions when you first begin.

At first, if you only have five minutes between one activity and the next, then use that time *in whatever way you can* to bring your awareness to the moment, and your intention to a devotional space. The length, frequency and quality of the time that you offer your spiritual practice *will shift on its own* as you begin to bring your desire for the shift to the front of your mind. You can trust that.

Awareness and Momentum

As we did with physical space, when working with chronological space at first you only want increased awareness and a little momentum. That is your simple, gentle start. Soon you will notice your Sovereign Soul beginning to rearrange your schedule for you to allow for greater expression and deeper receptivity. You can trust that too. You'll begin to realize that there is no lack of time in your schedule – you have the time, but you are using it for other things. Your priorities may need to be revised. A simple reprioritization of how you choose to spend the time that already exists is probably all you need. Ask yourself this – if there was a check for $10,000 waiting for you every time you took a half hour to spend doing something that connects you with your Soul, would you find the time? Probably. The issue is not availability of time, but what you think is important. *What you value.* The nearer you draw to your Sovereign Soul, the more you come to know and love her, the more you will begin to consciously examine how you are using the time that you have. You will begin to examine how you might gently approach shifting the use of that time to better align with your vision of a Soul-centered life.

Unique Challenges

Let's stop for a minute and take a look at why independent spiritual seekers might face unique challenges that seekers affiliated with organized religion do not. In most organized religions, there are prescribed times to explore devotional practices. Most religions have built devotional *routines* into specific aspects of the day, the week, the month, and the time of the year.

In addition to having a sound cyclical structure to rely upon, members of organized religions can be surrounded by fellow believers who are on the same spiritual schedule with the same routines in place. Structure, accountability and reinforcement are all built into each of the organized religious traditions and are available to any of their followers. And still, even with all that support, many truly devoted members of organized religions will continue to have trouble keeping the schedule, prioritizing the time and receiving the benefits of that structure, accountability and reinforcement. This is just part of what it means to be human.

Even under the best of circumstances, keeping a devotional practice alive and thriving in a world that does its best to distract and discourage you can be a huge challenge. No matter who you are, unless you live in a primarily spiritual community where the spiritual practice permeates all aspects of your day-to-day life, it is challenging to weave your internal spiritual practices into a life generally propelled by external forces. Jobs, bills, laws, friends, families, domestic duties, and social activities all crowd in and demand your attention. The truth is, you will have to choose and prioritize every single day and it will bring you face to face with your humanity all of your life. This challenge is just part of the basic experience of being a human, and it's not going to get any easier as time goes by and your distractions and responsibilities continue to grow exponentially.

So, as an independent spiritual seeker, you will face all of the same challenges that any seeker faces, but you will probably do it without the support of a spiritual community to prescribe a schedule, create accountability, keep you company and supply reinforcement when you take a detour. There will be times that it is going to feel like you are in this completely on your own with no support, but know now that that it is only an illusion. The more you move through the process and come to know your Sovereign Soul on deeper and deeper levels, the more resources you will discover to support you. For right now, all you have to do is show up. Show up and trust.

A Little Help, Please!

Remember that your development as a spiritual being is not just something your personal, conscious self wants to have. It is the prime directive of your magnificent Sovereign Soul. It is the reason that your Sovereign Soul exists. So you are now and will always be supported by her unwavering and incredibly powerful intention to manifest fully into your daily life. She has always been consistent in this purpose. She holds the answer to every challenge you meet. She creates the miracles that you believe you need to overcome whatever has held you captive all this time. She has both the power and the purpose to rearrange your entire life if necessary, in order to complete her mission and support your spiritual growth. You are definitely not alone.

Know that you are well supported and consistently inspired *even when you do not realize that you are.* Your Sovereign Soul will find the time or make the time she needs in order to fulfill her purpose. As the saying goes, you can do this the hard way or you can do this the easy way. You can align yourself with that purpose and consciously participate in shifting your priorities, or you can ignore the call, and the priorities will shift themselves, often not in ways that you would have chosen. Whatever gets it done.

If you want to make it easier on yourself, you may find it useful to really look at the role time plays in your life, the role you play in how you spend it, and how you can shift both to better align with your vision of a Soul-centered life. If you want to experience those shifts as satisfying and meaningful, it helps to be a full and willing participant in making them. So let's look at your life as it stands right now.

Time, Lifestyle and Priorities

The way your life looks right now is an exact reflection of your priorities. Your priorities drive your decisions and define how you choose to spend your time. Like an equation, you can see it from either direction. You can determine how you spend your time by looking at your priorities and the decisions that spring from those priorities, or, conversely, you can find out what your actual priorities are if you look at how you spend your time and what decisions you would have had to make in order to spend your time that way.

Here is the part where you probably protest (as we all do!) that a good many of your time-spending decisions are being made *for* you and that because you live in a society or have a family or hold down a job, you believe you have very little say in what you do with your time. From your perspective, the sensation at this point is anything *but* a feeling of having made (or even having *had*) a choice!

This is probably a persistent and compelling sensation for you. For example, it's hard to reason away the need to be employed, and with employment comes a whole set of rules around time and time expenditure that permeate the rest of your life even as you valiantly attempt to compensate for them. So your life as it stands right now is truthfully putting pressure both on you and on your time. You probably feel like you had very little, (if any), choice in the matter and nothing I am going to tell you is going to discount or invalidate that sensation. It is a very real sensation and a very convincing one, and I am not here to talk you out of it.

But as convincing as it is, it does have, tucked into the very heart of it, just a tiny little bit of built-in wiggle room. Just a little bit of flexibility, movement - some *give*. And that little bit of wiggle room is all you need. That wiggle room is where you begin.

The first little chink in the armor of your iron-clad, externally-dictated time schedule is, as it always is, awareness. It might surprise you to know that the way most of us actually spend time is usually a huge mystery to us. We write down where we think most of our time goes, but in keeping a log, we discover huge pockets of time that we spent but did not realize that we had spent. The first Wiggle Room is the room where we discover hidden time just by becoming aware of it.

This phenomenon is also true for money, so the first thing financial consultants will often ask you to do is to start keeping track of every penny you spend for a set period of time. This point is just to shine the light of your awareness on the huge blind spots in your perceptions of spending. Because the dynamic is identical for time, we are going to do the same thing here but with your time instead of your money.

As you begin to log your time, remember that perfection is not the goal. You are not shooting for 100% "useful" allocation of time. That would amount to a disheartening and unbalanced life. So this isn't about shame, blame, rigor, lack or deprivation. This is, and always was, only about discovery. There's a way to do this that feels good. There's a way to do it with love.

Down Time

The more time you spend observing and recording how you spend time, the more you will notice the cyclical nature of the way you spend it. You will go through periods of really potently useful time when your activities result in enrichment and great expansion of your spiritual growth, and then you will go through fallow periods where nothing you do seems to pay off, and you lose the thread entirely.

Every journey moves through these cycles of "on" and "off" times, and still, somehow, progress is made, people arrive at their destinations, and growth happens. What we forget is that the "off" times are as critical to the process as the "on" times, and many things can occur during "down time" that you are not even aware of. This concept is often difficult for the "productive" active rational western mind to contemplate and you may find yourself tempted to judge yourself during down time rather than simply accepting it. A lot can go on behind the scenes of your rational mind and your conscious agenda. Let's leave it at that for now.

Time Journaling

Take a specific period of time – no shorter than two weeks and no longer than a month, and begin to keep a time journal. At first it will feel like a pain to log every expenditure of time. You might be tempted to fudge the details. For instance, you might not want to log that hour you spent watching reality TV, or you might not want to record the three hours you spent on Facebook, when you think you should have been reading an *actual* book. You may not want to itemize that accidental nap you took after you put the kids down for their naps. In fact, you may surprise yourself by how much time slips right past you without your being aware of it, and, in response, you may be tempted to shame yourself for how you actually spent your time.

As you move deeper into the process you will begin to become aware (as we all do!) that there are huge chunks of time (interspersed between "required" activities) that seem either completely unproductive, or during which you are completely "checked out," and totally unaware that time is passing. Just keep logging your time expenditure as accurately and honestly as you can, and reserve judgment as much as possible. We are going back into that beginner's mind we talked about earlier, where you are only here to observe – not to make commentary or assessments. There will be plenty of time later on to review the habits, define the patterns and address any changes you want to make. For now, just observe and record. That's all you need to do.

Identifying and Realigning Priorities

Once you've given some attention to observing your habits and rituals around time, you'll be in a better position to find the Wiggle Room. When you really look at how you actually spend your time, you might find some really clear priorities lurking just behind your choices. Remind yourself at this point that there are no "right" or "wrong" priorities. Priorities are simply the *indicators of what we want* and what we want is usually just an *indicator of what we believe we need.* So more often than not the activity is not the point at all. Instead we are after whatever we think the activity offers. That's what really matters to us. That hidden agenda is the real priority.

For example, if I spend four hours on a beautiful sunny Sunday watching mindless television, my priority is not mindless television. When I ask myself the revealing question "If watching this program *were* useful, what use would it be?" I might receive the revealing answer "It keeps me company and it keeps me from noticing that I am lonely" or "It keeps my mind busy so that I don't get a chance to worry about my financial situation" or "It kills time until dinner so that I don't notice the laundry piling up and the dust bunnies under the couch." So under those answers you can hear that the priority might actually be comfort, or company, or distraction. It could really be anything. But hidden behind every activity is a pay-off of some kind. Whatever the pay-off is, *that pay-off is your real priority*. So the second bit of Wiggle Room comes with getting to the root of the need, and then finding some other way to meet it that aligns with your Sovereign Soul's purpose.

Meeting Your Real Needs

Every activity will either enrich you or not. Obviously there's a spectrum there, but you can tell when you leave an activity better for having participated in it, or when you leave it "worse off" than before you started it. This is a really key concept for you to get, because it is the secret power in the second Wiggle Room. Once you know why you are doing something you can find a more enriching way to do it that still meets your real need.

For most of us, meeting the perceived need is not negotiable. We'll work out a way to meet the need before it ever reaches our conscious decision-making mind. So ignoring a need only makes that need go underground and when it does, it leaves you powerless to decide the best way to meet it. Instead, you're left with whatever is most handy and seems least threatening to the status quo.

When you discover what the need is, and stop fighting it – when you find a positive, enriching way to meet it instead, then you begin to align your activities and priorities with your vision of a Soul-centered life. That's when you become available to work in partnership with your Sovereign Soul to create that life.

Know that whatever enriches you, by definition feeds your Soul. Whatever does not enrich you, by definition ignores your

Soul. This is true, but it doesn't make those activities "good" and "bad" so try to stay out of the impulse to judge them. Come back to the position of the neutral observer. You're not trying to judge the activities, but instead you just want to see what's true for you right now. You're on a mission of discovery.

You cannot discover a real need (or meet that need) when you are asking questions from a position of shame or blame. This exercise is only about finding out what your priorities are, and then tracing them back to your real needs. This is not about picking the "good priorities" and weeding out the "bad priorities." Your Wiggle Room right now lies in your finding out the truth about how you are actually spending your time and why. If you are going to beat yourself up for what you find there, then you are never going to get to the truth. So suspend your judgment and ask your questions without fear of retribution. If you pay with your attention, you will be rewarded with your truth.

Once you've identified your priorities and uncovered the real needs they were meeting, the next task is to identify which needs are being met in a manner that enriches you and aligns with your Soul-centered life.

The Higher Order

Take a deep breath here because you don't have to enrich your Sovereign Soul every second of every day. Not every minute of every "non-enrichment" activity has to be eliminated and not every minute of enrichment has to be expanded. Remember, you are completely free. Your Sovereign Soul is operating from an agenda that is well beyond the idea of "should" and "has to" and you are answering to *that* agenda. Your Soul is operating from a higher order. Words like "should" and "have to" are limited and limiting words and your Soul abides no limitation. Most of all you need to remember that because you are operating under this higher order, there is nothing that you "have to" do. You are free to choose. As you work with time, the goal is really to bring your freedom of choice back to you, and to make you consciously aware of those choices. So take a deep breath.

Now, some things you choose to do will make your life easier, more satisfying, more comfortable and more harmonious. Those things enrich you and strengthen your connection to the Divine. Other things you choose to do will make you numb, and lower your energy. They will seem to disconnect you from Source, fragment your attention and grind you down physically. These things do not enrich you and they do not enhance your connection to the Divine, *but neither do they eliminate it.* Your Sovereign Soul, the Divine impulse within you, remains strong and whole regardless of your behavior. Regardless of your choices. The only thing that suffers is your *perception* of being connected to that impulse – your ability to *experience* it!

Going to the River

To illustrate this, imagine that the Divine is a river of clean, clear water running past you, right there for you to drink from. You can spend your time walking towards it, or you can spend your time sitting, staring at it, or you can turn your back and sit facing another direction doing your level best to drown out the sound of it bubbling along merrily behind you.

At some times you will feel more thirsty than you do at others. If you hum a lot, and cover your ears, you may at times manage to put it out of your mind. But you have not harmed the river by ignoring it, and nor have you eliminated or even minimized its availability to you. At any point you can stand up, turn around and walk toward it. You can get down on your knees and cup your hands and scoop up that clear cool water and drink fully from it. You can take off your clothes, fold them neatly, place them on a warm rock in the sun, and wade, naked, into the refreshing water any time you want.

None of these versions of the story are any better or worse than the others. It's just that some are so very much more pleasant, and refreshing, and nourishing than the others. There is no course of action that you "should" take, or "must" take to "find" your Sovereign Soul. There are just those that bring you more and more closely and frequently into contact with it, from staring at it, to moving toward it, to kneeling before it, to taking it in, drinking from it, and finally to immersing yourself in it completely.

When you look at the activities with which you fill your time, you will see those activities falling along much the same spectrum of connection that I've described in this metaphor. All we want to do right now is ask the question: "When I do <whatever activity> where does it put me in relation to the river (my Sovereign Soul)? " Next to each activity in the log you've been keeping, write where down your intuitive sense about where it puts you. Some examples are below:

C&#x03; When I am making love I am completely naked, immersed in the river and swimming.

C&#x03; When I am eating, I am sitting, facing the river in the sun.

C&#x03; When I am watching TV, I am asleep at the edge of the forest. I can hear the river but I cannot see it.

C&#x03; When I smoke a cigarette, I am walking slowly into the forest away from the river.

C&#x03; When I pray I am kneeling at the edge of the river, and drinking fully, holding my hair back with my hands, and drinking right out of the water with my face immersed.

ଔ When I am listening to music that uplifts me, I have removed my socks and shoes and I am sitting on a flat rock at the edge of the river, dangling my feet in it, feeling it moving, cool and refreshing all around me. I cannot hear anything at that point but the rush of the river.

This should give you an example of a way to look at the activities without passing judgment on them, or discouraging yourself. There is nothing inherently wrong with walking slowly into a forest away from a river, but I can always turn around and walk back. Neither approach is forcing my hand, but one may be more appealing than the other. So I can evaluate it from the standpoint of what, in this image, is more appealing.

I can, in the moment, *any moment*, take a different approach, follow a different impulse, make a different choice. And the locus of power, the impetus, is mine and mine alone. It does not belong to "Should" but instead rests firmly in the hands of "Could" who may at any second pass it on to "Would," - you never know. So this exercise is your next step.

When you have completed your evaluation, you will be able to see clearly the following things: What you do with your time, why you do those things with your time, and how doing that with your time affects you, spiritually. Now it is time to take a step back. You have done a lot of work and you are more aware, and now more free because of that awareness, than you have been for a while. It can be overwhelming.

So now is not the time to lunge forward with a hard charge straight into the wheels of change. You've gone gently so far, and you will continue to go gently, because your Soul has all the time in the world. She isn't going anywhere and she has infinite patience. To align yourself fully with your vision of a Soul-centered life, you are going to have to practice a little patience yourself. So the next step is actually a step back. Before you proceed, let's look at how much time is ample time.

The Nature of Time

Time is a strange thing. You can do a thing, over and over, every single day for ten years and barely notice you are doing it until somebody points it out to you. Or you can do something once, suddenly, for a very brief moment, and the impact of that moment can resonate with you for the rest of your life. Both quality and quantity of time are variables that can influence the impact any period of time can have on your life.

We pay a great deal of attention to the quantity of time necessarily, mostly because the culture encourages us to do so, but also because it is easier to measure and to account for. However, you will find that it is the *quality* of time that can propel a brief moment from obsolescence to immortality. The quality of the time is what makes an impression on you. So when you ask yourself "How much time is enough time to connect with my Soul?" you are not asking a simple question with a simple answer.

Quality Time

When you ask that question, you have just opened a fantastic portal into the third and most powerful of all the Wiggle Rooms in our schedule. The key to this particular Wiggle Room is this: "the *quantity* of time required to create a lasting impact is directly proportionate to the *quality* of that time spent." Simple. If you do something by rote, methodically, with little attention or intention, then it will take a much longer time for that thing to benefit you. On the other hand, if you give your full attention to it, and do it full out, no holds barred, with all of your energy, your heart and soul, then you only need do it briefly in order to get the same impact, and only slightly longer in order to get an even greater impact. This holds true, by the way, of everything.

Physical exercise is a prime example. If you go to the gym and you climb onto the elliptical machine, flip open a magazine and distractedly read several articles while completing your thirty minute regime, your body will have one experience of exercise. If you climb onto the same machine, put some music on, close your eyes and bring your attention to all the muscles of your body, specifically working the problem areas, concentrating on your form as you do the exercise, working with your breath to create the optimal conditions for receiving the benefits, both your body and your mind will have a completely different experience of exercise and the amplified effect on both will be substantial. This is the difference, literally, between going through the motions and bringing your "A" Game. The same holds true for a spiritual practice. A few, very focused, very attentive, and very devoted minutes will trump an hour of half-hearted, hurried efforts.

That being said, it should also be remembered that spiritual growth, like any growth, does require time and patience. There are now, and probably will always be long periods where it seems like nothing is happening, and then sudden moments of breakthrough and insight. So no spiritual practice can subsist purely on a few stolen yet powerfully focused moments. Balance is key.

Experimenting with Balance

If you can strike a balance between the two approaches to time, that would be ideal. Allow for some of your practice to consist of brief, but completely focused moments, squeezed in wherever you can, whenever you can and then don't worry about it. Do it full out, 100%, for whatever brief time you have available, and then let it do its work on you behind the scenes throughout the rest of your day and week.

Also try fully committing to several long stretches of uninterrupted time, when you have the luxury of simply allowing whatever needs to happen, happen during that time. Approach the time loosely, with curiosity, instead of being propelled by the intention or the power of pure focus that fueled the brief moments we talked about earlier.

During these longer, uninterrupted times, you can turn control of your spiritual practice over to your Sovereign Soul, and see what emerges. You have created a cushion around these blocks of time, so that you don't feel rushed. You don't need to assert your will during these times. You are there to receive. You are there to allow. That's all that's required – stay present and allow.

So you can probably feel that these are two very different qualities of time; two different ways of approaching and participating with time. On a small scale it defines how you see yourself, and your role within that period of time, but on a much larger scale it can change how you see time itself. When you work with the quality of time, you begin to understand on a visceral level that time (like physical space) can consist of very different environments. A laser-focused moment is a very different environment than a diffused, welcoming, receptive moment. And you can choose from moment to moment which environment best serves to align you with your Soul-centered life.

You may have noticed that the quality of the time seems to be determined by your intention for that space of time, and in these two examples, this is indeed the case. You show up to these "spiritual appointments" with a specific goal in mind, and when you do, the goal informs the environment in which it can take place. But this is not always the case.

Time and Emotion

Sometimes the quality of the time can be determined by other influences. For instance, sometimes your emotional state will influence the quality of the time you spend. I'll give you an example. In one situation, you are rushing to the airport to catch a plane. You have five minutes to get there, and while the traffic seems to slow down, the minutes seem to fly by. You are anxious and getting more so. The more anxious you get, the slower the traffic moves in relation to the minutes ticking by. You have the sensation that time passed very, very quickly, and it was not a pleasant sensation to feel so helpless and rushed.

In the second situation, you are having a wonderful date with a new love interest you find fascinating. You eat dinner, and afterwards go for a walk on the wharf overlooking the city lights. Before you know it, hours have flown by and it is time to go home. Where did the time go? It just seemed to fly by. Indeed, in this situation you also had the sensation that time passed very, very quickly, because you were so engaged in the dynamic with your new romantic interest. But you felt happy, and excited and caught up in the moment all night. At no time did you feel helpless or rushed. So this illustrates how time passing by very quickly can be interpreted either as a negative or a positive experience, depending upon the emotional state you bring to it.

One dimension to the quality of time is the perceived speed with which it passes. An entirely different dimension to the quality of time is the emotional state you bring to it, and although this seems like something over which you have control, in many cases it is not, for all intents and purposes. And really, that isn't even the point. We could spend a while talking about how there are productive states of mind and less productive or even destructive states of mind, but the real practical truth is that your Sovereign Soul wants your presence, exactly as it is. Exactly as you are.

Come As You Are

Trying to "fix" your state of mind before you approach your spiritual practice, is a little like the woman who cleans her whole house before the maid comes. Your Sovereign Soul is best equipped and most adept at receiving you in whatever emotional state you may find yourself when you arrive and using whatever it is that you've brought with you to deepen the trust and connection that you experience. So don't waste any time trying to talk yourself out of your feelings before you turn to Spirit. Instead, just come as you are, and notice how that changes your experience and impacts the nature of the time spent in practice. Again, you are going gently through this. Your Sovereign Soul is vast and spacious. She can use any quality of time that you are willing to spend with her. There is room for all of it, so come as you are.

Making the Subtle Shift

Remember the evaluation that you did of how you spent your time? You made a detailed log of your time, and then evaluated each of the activities in the log in terms of what it offered you (what was the payoff?) and how doing those activities for those payoffs was impacting you on a spiritual level. You looked at what was enriching, and what was depleting. Now you return to your evaluation with fresh eyes.

Feed What Works

The first thing to do is to notice what you are doing right. We've discussed momentum before, and here you will find the same dynamic: it will be easier for you to expand upon nourishing activities that you are *already* doing than it would be to eliminate activities that do not nourish you. So right off the bat the focus now is to pour some conscious attention into the activities that you're already doing and that you have recognized as Soul satisfying.

You will probably begin to notice that once you've identified an activity as enriching, that activity will become more and more prominent in your schedule, and other activities that meet the same need will also show up and become obvious. This is the dynamic of *collateral encouragement*. The more time and attention you devote to a particular quality or environment, the more all the things that *align* with that environment will begin to appear. You have created the condition internally that supports that endeavor or approach. So take notice of these effects as you journal. Notice what the attendant activities and behaviors are that accompany that subtle shift.

Once you've cultivated a little momentum and strengthened the role of Soul-satisfying activities in your schedule, it's time to look at some of the old, less satisfying aspects of your schedule.

Less satisfying activities will be those you've identified as meeting a need of yours, but doing it in a way that doesn't support your connection to your Sovereign Soul. Dedication of time to this activity has been at least partially useful to you, so far, but you can see that by the time you finish the activity you are less healthy, less happy, less fulfilled than you were when you first began. You may notice that whether or not you actually enjoy or like the activity, the net result is a lowering of your energy, your outlook, and your feelings of being connected, or "tuned in" to your Sovereign Soul.

Because of the work that you did earlier, you probably already know why you do the activity. You have identified a very clear payoff or series of payoffs that come with that activity and that keep you coming back to it. Today we will look at different ways to get those payoffs without committing so much time to that particular activity.

Eventually you may find that you can meet that need so completely in a different way that the activity itself simply disappears from your routine, effortlessly. Other times you may need to exert some discipline to make a choice that brings you more into alignment with your Soul-centered life over one that seems to limit that alignment. This, as usual, will be a dance. You will move in and out of clarity and purpose with this, but the exercise, and the awareness will continue to increase. As your ability to address these issues in a conscious way grows, your choices will become easier as well.

Your body's natural state is health, and it constantly yearns to return to that state. It does everything that it can to bring you back to health when you are ill, even when you may continue to do things that work against that effort. Your valiant, beautiful body continues to try to return to health.

That's how it is with your Sovereign Soul. Your natural state is total union with your Sovereign Soul all day, every day of your life. Your Soul knows this, and she will continue to assist and support you as you make your way more and more into alignment and union with her. You can trust her. Your well-being, spiritually and in every way, is her only mission.

Eliminating Barrier Activities

To begin with, simply choose one activity, perhaps the one that you are the least attached to. Spend some time journaling around that activity – notice when you are most likely to do that activity and what conditions are in place at the time to support you in doing that activity. Describe the payoff in great, rich detail. Really get into the heart of the payoff, because that is where the juice is. That's the *real* reason you do what you do.

Now, think about other ways you might get exactly that payoff, but in a way that also supports your spiritual growth. Invite your Soul into the discussion, and sit with the question. Remind yourself that *you do not need to surrender the payoff.* In whatever way you are being comforted or rewarded for this activity, you can continue to be comforted and rewarded. You will not be asked to give up comfort or reward. You will only be asked to consider alternate ways to comfort yourself or reward yourself, perhaps even more. At first you may want to simply experiment with other ways, not surrendering the original model, but trying on a few different ones in addition to the first. This way you give up nothing.

It may be useful for me to give you some examples, so let's start with an easy one: television. Many of us use television for a variety of reasons. It keeps us company, it provides a rhythm to our chores, it takes our minds off of things we would rather not think about, it keeps us in touch with the outside world, it makes us feel as though we have alternate lives than the ones we are living by fantasizing about them on our behalf, it kills time, it makes us laugh, and it gives us something to look forward to on a regular basis. For many of us, the idea of living in a home without a television is tantamount to a stint in prison.

Even contemplating a home without a TV can make us uncomfortable, and if we think about it more deeply, it feels almost like losing a member of the family. The television has taken on such a central role in our lives that it has become the hearth; the thing that we gather around at the end of the day, the reward that we give ourselves for doing the things we don't want to do.

Most of us would not, however, describe the time spent watching television as time that brings us closer to our Sovereign Soul or brings us into deeper and deeper union with the Divine. It may try to fulfill those functions but instead it leaves us over-stimulated, sometimes agitated and even worse, often "checked out" or numb. None of these collateral states have any value in terms of deepening our connection to the Divine or aligning with our vision of a Soul-centered life.

The mission, should you choose to accept it of course, is to look at each of those fulfilled or partially fulfilled needs and experiment with alternate ways to meet them. If a habit (such as television viewing) meets many needs, be gentle in your approach, experimenting with meeting the needs one at a time.

This is not the time to go "cold turkey" or you will simply create a vacuum.

A good visual for this style of implementing change is the image of a glass of dirty water. All you need to do is to start a trickle of clean water into the glass and little by little the dirty water will be removed and replaced by the pure water, with no pain and hardly any effort on your part.

So in our example of television viewing, rather than tossing the TV out the front door, you would simply take one of the needs that the TV meets (company, for example) and play around with some alternate ways to give yourself company. This would be a gradual shift, taken fully in the spirit of play. You might experiment with leaving some music playing when you go out, so that there is already music, or a favorite radio station on when you get home, creating a sense of greeting. Or you might invest in a series of audio books, or language learning CDs, and have those at the ready when you arrive.

At first it almost doesn't matter how else you meet that need, as long as you bring your conscious awareness to it, and you are willing to give it a try, even for a short period of time. Little by little, these more healthy, more spiritually aligned choices will build momentum, and all without the need for you to exert a lot of effort and force to eliminate the old habit. This is almost a *spiritually economic approach* – if you have honestly identified your needs and you are actually meeting them, then your personality doesn't have to go out and meet them some other way. The only real effort is in the creativity you bring to the table and your willingness to initiate the experiment.

Journal as Secret Weapon

It should be obvious, by now, that your journal will become (if it hasn't already!) a daily companion on your journey to a Soul-centered life. Think of your journal as your secret weapon. Your journal will chronicle your explorations, offering you the space and time and attention that make all the difference. So as you unravel the hold your habits have on your time, let your journal guide you, and keep you focused. Use the pages as an opportunity to sit with each question for a while, let it sink in, explore possibilities, expand upon inspirations, make lists, or describe solutions and situations in great detail. If you are inspired by a lyric, or a quote, or something you heard someone say in an elevator, jot it down. You'll be surprised how often your Soul speaks to you that way. Let your journal help you to flesh out the journey, reveal insights, and keep track of your progress as you go. You've heard it before, but I'll say it again - a life worth living is a life worth journaling.

The Most Important Questions Right Now

So, what are the most important questions you should you ask yourself as you begin this process? The following is certainly not a comprehensive list, but it will get you engaged in the process, and call out the creative elements of your being as you address the challenge at hand.

- ⋈ What needs does this habit/activity meet?

- ⋈ How well does it meet those needs?

- ⋈ How can I tell when the need has been met?

- ⋈ Do I normally stop engaging in the activity when the need has been met?

- ⋈ Has the need *ever* been fully met? How?

- ⋈ Has it been partially met? How?

- ⋈ What other things do I do in my daily routine that already meet that need?

- ⋈ What percentage of my day is spent meeting that need?

- ⋈ How do I feel after I am done with this activity?

- ⋈ Do I ever stop the activity before I have met the need?

- ⋈ What is it, specifically about this activity that meets the need?

03 How do I feel about the need itself?

03 What activities can I imagine myself doing that seem like they could also meet the need?

03 What barriers (if any) stand between me and engaging in those activities as well?

03 Are the barriers (if any) real, or imaginary (something I think could become a barrier, but have not actually tried, so I don't know for sure).

03 What would I have to put into place to experiment with these other activities?

03 What small thing can I do right now, today, as soon as I put this pen down, to start that ball rolling – to get the experiment underway?

These are the kinds of questions you will want to journal about as you feel your way closer and closer to a more spiritually satisfying solution for meeting a particular need. The next step, of course, would be to do that one small thing, right now, today, as soon as you put the pen down that will start the ball rolling.

Bring your own creativity together with the guidance of your Sovereign Soul to find a healthy, fulfilling activity that can meet the need you are working on even better than you had been able to meet it before. As you experiment with these new choices, record your successes, record your frustrations, record anything and everything that the journey brings to you. Journaling will amplify your ability to understand the changes that you are implementing, to experience the changes fully and to expedite your shift.

When All Things Become Prayer

I want to bring your attention, now, back to the nature of time and the Sovereign Soul. Volumes and volumes have been written about time and time management. While I've suggested some alternate ways to look at time, and some new ways to think about how you personally relate to time, and why you are "spending" time in the way that you are spending it, the ultimate purpose of this chapter is not to get you to change how you spend your time, or even to change how you understand time.

The ultimate purpose of this chapter is to bring your awareness to how your Sovereign Soul understands time. You and your beautiful Soul have only one dynamic, and that dynamic is *relationship*. Every second of every minute of every day of your life, you are and always have been in relationship with your Sovereign Soul. Like any relationship, there are times when you are more connected to and immersed in the relationship than at other times. So this chapter, although it addresses the nature of time, is really a chapter about relationship.

From the vantage point of your Sovereign Soul, every second of your life is a prayer. Every activity, every thought, every choice that you make is a prayer. The nature of your prayer changes with the things that you do, the thoughts that you think and the choices that you make. It changes with how you feel and what you intend as you move through your day. But no matter what you are doing, or thinking or choosing or feeling, you continue to pray. It's just that sometimes you don't know you are praying. Or you aren't praying on purpose. But the living of your life IS a prayer. It never stops being one. And your Sovereign Soul knows this. She hears your constant prayers. So what are you praying? Do you even know?

Since the dawn of time, mystics have been working toward the state of enlightenment, when they can perceive and receive the Divine in everything all the time. It is worthwhile, then, to remember that enlightenment is only a matter of perception. The only thing that has changed in the being when she becomes enlightened, is that that she can now *perceive* the Divine in every moment.

The Divine hasn't changed at all. The Divine was always present in every moment. And the mystic has always been relating to the Divine in every moment. That hasn't changed either. The only thing that has changed is the mystic's ability to *perceive* that relationship. So, right now, as unenlightened as you, or I or anybody is, we are still praying every moment. We are still relating to the Divine. We are still reaching out to the essential spiritual nature of life and we are still communicating. And the relationship shifts for us when we are communicating in a loving, open, receptive and hopeful way.

The Divine does not change depending upon our approach, but we do. We change. So we may not see God in everything we do, but God sees us. The relationship we experience with God, or with our own Sovereign Soul, and with the essential Divinity that surrounds us, will change for us as we begin to perceive it more and more often. It is then that we will change how we pray. We will change *what* we pray.

So right now, reading this book, you are praying. You may be praying relief. You may be praying hope. You may be praying joy. You may be praying frustration or confusion, but you are praying. And, as you pray, your relationship with and your ability to relate to the Divine changes too.

Letting Love Flourish

I don't want you to come away from this chapter thinking that your Sovereign Soul wants you to shape up and manage your time better. That's not it at all. Your Sovereign Soul wants your relationship with her to flourish. The quality of your prayers will let that happen, if you want it to happen.

Approach the changes in how you spend your time from this position – that you do not want to cut back, or knock off, or whip anything into shape. You want something to flourish. You want it to blossom, to be vital, to be beautiful. And you want your prayers to be those things as well. Seek, now, only to see the way you spend your time through *those* eyes, the eyes of prayer, the eyes of Love. As you become more and more aware throughout your day that your life *is* your prayer, you will find yourself releasing the things that keep you from truly living your Soul-centered life and you will do it peacefully, effortlessly. The prayer that is your life will become a prayer of joy and wonder, a prayer of hope. And that is a Soul-centered life.

Chapter Four
Cultivating Profound Privacy

Developing a spiritual practice requires more than just time and space. It requires a profound sense of privacy. The more deeply you enter this journey, the more intimate the journey becomes. At first, you will find yourself eager to reach out to others. So much of what you are exploring will feel new, and fresh and vital to you. So much of what you are feeling will almost burst out of you, because you are on a path of discovery and discovery begs to be shared.

There will be moments of confusion on your journey, and you will find yourself wanting to check in with other people, get some feedback, maybe to regain your bearings. Each of these impulses will spring from a natural sense of having deeply connected, having experienced something and wanting to share that experience, wanting to solidify it as you share it with others.

But the spiritual journey is a profoundly intimate one. The more you open to the Divine, and the more you let your Sovereign

Soul speak to and through you, the less you will be able to conceal, either from yourself or from others. You will necessarily learn about cultivating the respect that your relationship with the Divine deserves, and you will come to understand, perhaps through painful experiences, the wisdom of maintaining a sense of profound privacy around your journey. The more you are able to do these two things, the more deeply you will engage with your Sovereign Soul and the more powerfully her presence will impact you.

Why Privacy?

The most important reason to cultivate a culture of respect and privacy around your spiritual journey is that your relationship (both with yourself and with the Divine) will be in a state of flux. You'll be spiritually open and vulnerable as you explore previously unknown territories and you'll find yourself asking questions you've never asked before. It's crucial at this point to create a protected space, both physically, and emotionally, for this kind of exploration.

You will be challenged, internally, on levels that you've not experienced before and you'll need to feel secure enough to do that. You cannot feel secure if you feel that you must defend every choice, every experiment, every approach and idea that you entertain. Other people in your life may automatically resist any change on your part. There will be some who appear to applaud your efforts, but most humans (no matter how evolved) prefer stasis to change, especially as it relates to their relationships with other humans.

Some people will seek to support you but may do so from within the context of their own filters and assumptions. This could make it difficult for them to tolerate any uncertainty on your part. When you sound hesitant, their own discomfort may cause them to rush forward with a certainty of their own to try and fill the vacuum. They may be equally uncomfortable with any new certainties that you bring to the mix. Some people will automatically rise up in response with their own certainty when they hear yours. People can sometimes be pretty predictable when confronted with change in one another.

People who are following their own spiritual path may actively attempt to counter your explorations. If they are following a tradition that embraces the concept of conversion, they may intuitively recognize your openness and your willingness to reach out and, however well-meaningly, attempt to bring you into the fold. If they are not engaged in a formal spiritual tradition, they will probably be very eager to share their insights and to debate where their insights differ from yours. This will not be malicious in any way, simply a natural byproduct of the independent seeker. We are all eager to engage wherever and however we can with others on the path.

Either way, now may not be the appropriate time for you to be sharing every little thing. There will be some things that you would do well to explore in the company of other like-minded seekers, and there will be other things that were meant only for you; things that are not up for debate. These ideas will need your protection in order to have time to fully develop. In time you will learn to distinguish between the two and how to tell a healthy opportunity for communion from a potentially toxic exchange.

Ready to Share

Another thing you will learn to recognize is when an idea or insight becomes ready for sharing. Some wisdom is tender and takes a while to settle into your consciousness. Until it "sets," it remains vulnerable to external influences and to potentially harmful exchanges. Once it has taken root and begun to really manifest itself in your daily life, you will begin to interact with a new concept or experience on a variety of levels. When it eventually becomes a part of who you are on a daily basis, then it will be sturdy enough to withstand the exposure that comes with sharing new ideas with other people.

You will begin to become aware of that readiness, and when you do it will feel like you cannot contain it a minute longer without sharing. It will become something that people know about you because of the way you are living, rather than it being something you have to tell them. Being able to sense the difference between an idea that is truly ready to be shared, and one that you are desperate to share simply because it is new and you crave validation, is a skill that will serve you well in every area of your life, not just spiritually.

Private Places

It may seem obvious, but in order to maintain privacy around your practice, you will have to discover or create a physical space in which you can explore privately. You will need an actual location or locations in which you can feel comfortable to fully engage in your spiritual practice without an audience. These places must be physically secure, in the sense that they should be set apart from public space where you can create things (a journal, art, an altar) without fear of interruption or prying eyes.

If you live alone, this is relatively easy to accomplish, but, if you live with others as most of us do, you may find this significantly challenging. Some practical work-arounds may include creating a mobile space (something that you can set up and dismantle with relative ease) or creating or purchasing a container that is secure (such as a lockable desk, or cabinet), in a room with a door that you can lock. When you engage in your spiritual pursuits, you can lock the door behind you to avoid interruptions, and unlock your cabinet to reveal your supplies and your altar. These are both reasonable solutions.

The third solution you might want to try is to remodel or revamp a space like a garage, or a shed, or basement so that it becomes specifically your space for spiritual practice. Give this some thought, and some time and attention in your journal to find the best solution for you.

Remember, as always, that it doesn't have to be perfect, it just has to create an opening, some way for you to show up and to feel safe in doing so. One last consideration, as far as physical privacy goes, that you may want to think about if you live with others is how you will handle privacy as it relates to noise.

Noise and Privacy

Your practice may involve vocalized prayer, chanting, sometimes weeping, sometimes singing, all things that most of us would rather not do publicly, or, at a very minimum, certainly not in front of those who do not share similar activities and interests. As hard as you try, it will be impossible to completely insulate the noises of your spiritual practice from the outside world (just ask any musician who has tried to create a studio in their home). It can be challenging.

The advantage you may have over the musician is that you do not usually require an entire studio to complete your practice. You can do it anywhere, which leaves you free to do it in the car, in the shower, or simply when nobody else is at home. As you progress on this journey and you become familiar with the ways in which sound plays a part in your practice, you will devise the methods and means by which to accommodate them.

In the meantime, it may be useful for you to include some sort of masking sounds in your private space. This can take the form of a white noise-maker outside the door (such as they use in therapists' offices) and/or a CD player to play spiritually uplifting music during your alone time with your Sovereign Soul. Both are somewhat effective and will support your sense of safety and privacy as you engage in your practice.

Alone Time

A collateral, but equally essential component of a truly private spiritual practice is actual "alone time" with your Sovereign Soul. Finding or creating this can be as challenging for the independent mystic as securing a physical private space. Let's be candid; there is nothing in our modern world today that either reinforces or even encourages time spent alone with Spirit. Unless a seeker belongs to an organized religion, every aspect of modern living will actively discourage the simple act of sitting down, alone, in spiritual pursuit.

The simplest way to approach this challenge and truly begin a spiritual practice is to schedule the time, the way you would schedule anything. Put it on the calendar, set your cell phone alarm clock, and get into the habit of going there. Although simple (and hardly romantic!) this is a very powerful strategy for a number of reasons.

First, it insists that you do not need to be in a perfectly spiritual mood in order to embark upon the practice. It allows you to "come as you are." This sounds simple but will be critical because you are now beginning to *form an association between your practice and the conditions that precipitate it*. If you start off waiting for the perfect state of mind to practice, then you will develop an association to that state of mind as a precipitant. If you show up, no matter what state of mind you're in, you will prove that you can be present and experience value no matter what state of mind you're in. Second, this strategy lets you plan the time around the schedules of any other people you may live with so that you can ensure optimal privacy. And third, it ensures that you will approach your practice from a variety of personal states, which allows your Sovereign Soul to engage with you in a variety of ways. This keeps you from getting too hung up on the details, and gives you the broadest opportunity to engage with your beloved Soul.

It will be helpful, probably at first, if you can devise a set of rewards (bribes!) for yourself, just for the first 21 days, long enough to get in the habit of making the time. Go out and purchase 21 small, inexpensive gifts – little luxuries that you really want. Then reward yourself with one on each day that you keep your practice schedule. Once you begin to get into the habit of the daily practice, and it starts to become an intrinsic part of the whole rhythm of your day, then you will not need to reward yourself. The practice itself will become your reward. But in the beginning, sweeten the pot. Why not?

Conceptual Privacy

Now that we've established the physical, practical privacy considerations, it is time to address the more esoteric or conceptual ones. A spiritual journey requires that the seeker erect a barrier of secrecy around new ideas and insights for a pre-set period of time, or what I call "conceptual privacy". This initial secrecy fulfills two needs – firstly, it frees you to explore without judgment from others, which allows you to show up as authentically as possible. To better understand this, imagine how different your journal entries would be if you knew, while you were writing them, that you were going to have to read them aloud to an audience the next day. Until you become secure in the knowledge that you will protect your own privacy, you will not allow yourself be truly authentic, even when you are alone. You can only afford to tell yourself the truth when you have proven to yourself that you can be trusted. Secondly, it allows the deeply personal nature of your relationship with your Sovereign Soul to take root in the most intimate way possible.

Intimacy and Commitment

It is impossible to overestimate the intensely intimate nature of spiritual pursuit. If you have come this far down the path and you are still unaware that this journey is not a superficial one, then you had best go back to the beginning and contemplate your involvement in it at all. As harsh as that sounds, this journey is impossible to make, safely, on your own, without commitment. And further, it is impossible to truly serve Love, the love between you and your Sovereign Soul, if you are not able to commit to it.

You cannot be committed to Love if you are not willing to be authentic, vulnerable and real in the face of it. If you have tried to sally forth, dabbling here and there, and not really even getting your feet wet, then this may not be the time for you. The seeker on this path will be guided, as a lover is guided, into ever more intimate circumstances and revelations. You must be committed enough and available enough emotionally to follow that guidance.

The Sovereign Soul has always been fully aware of what and who you are. It is you who are not yet fully aware of your essential self. If you are not willing to *become* aware of your most true self, then you will not be able to navigate this terrain. Your commitment and your willingness to allow yourself to be truly vulnerable with yourself are what hold your wheels to the cart and the cart to the road. So, from a spiritual perspective, your safety as an independent seeker relies most wholeheartedly upon your authenticity. The path will make you real if you would let it, and being real requires privacy, intimacy and respect.

The version of you that will engage in this level of exploration demands that you respect the inherent vulnerability of that state, and requires that you keep confidential whatever transpires between you and your Soul for at least as long as it takes to let the concepts mature and begin to express themselves in your daily life. Conceptual privacy is a covenant you make with yourself to hold all confidences confidential and to recognize them as sacred, and therefore precious. This is the old "pearls before the swine" concept, (not to put too fine a point on it...) and as you teach yourself respect for the gifts that your Sovereign Soul shares with you, you also strengthen the portal through which they arrive. Simply put, the more secure the container, the more likely it is to receive the treasure. So, conceptual privacy both welcomes new ideas and allows them to gestate in a safe, protected space.

Keeping Your Own Counsel

You don't have to tell everyone everything all the time. We've already talked about not sharing ideas before their time, but we haven't talked about it in terms of "keeping your own counsel." This is a very powerful stance that you can take, in which you determine exactly how much of yourself to reveal to any particular setting or audience. We all do this to some degree automatically, but few of us approach it consciously from a point of choice.

Imagine for a moment the nun or the monk that has taken a vow of silence. There are many reasons to take such a vow, many motivators at play, but for our purposes, let's look only at the outcome of such a vow. This will help to make a distinction between Conceptual Privacy (protecting ideas by keeping them contained within a sacred space) and Keeping Your Own Counsel (protecting yourself by not letting toxic energy and ideas into your sacred inner space).

We can all agree that certainly not every thought that the nun is having is a profoundly private one, yet her silence creates around her an air of mystery. That air of mystery protects her from intrusion by external forces and ideas. It is impossible to argue with someone under a vow of silence. So essentially, it is a choice not to disengage, but *to engage on a different level*; a level that is receptive, yet protective.

A person under a vow of silence is engaging in a primarily receptive stance, but, much like the Aikido masters, is allowing what is potentially confrontational, or threatening to glide right past her. So, although she may be supremely receptive, she is protected by her silence as well. Simply put, the circuit, on the brute level, has not been made. Relative to energetic exchanges, words could be considered "brute" forces. Because the nun has not "volleyed" the words back at those speaking around her, she remains immune from any of the more coarse, or base ways in which we engage.

I am not suggesting that you take a vow of silence, mind you, but I do want to highlight the energetic dynamics of the verbal exchange, and to show you very clearly how powerful a tool silence can be to protect your inner space and create the profound privacy that your journey will require. I am recommending that you experiment with silence as you interact with others, so that you can feel the impact firsthand.

Incremental Silence

Silence has power even in tiny increments. For example, if you sense that a person is beginning to become either agitated or intrusive with you, you can simply practice responding slowly to the individual, taking a full three to five counts of silence before you even open your mouth. You need not speak slowly, just insert these tiny spacers in between each sentence, creating small moments of silence in between each communication. You will be amazed at how powerful this can be when you experiment with it. Almost immediately you will notice the other person slowing down as well. You will find your thoughts, when you do speak, will come more clearly and concisely. Even tiny "vows" of silence can purify (for lack of a better word!) a communication or series of communications. Silence is purifying. It acts as a filter for all that passes through it.

Other Choices for Silence

There are many other ways in which you can choose to maintain your privacy through silence. You can choose not to engage in specific conversations that seem intrusive or toxic to your development. You can choose to take five minutes day to actively practice silence, even when surrounded by people. You can create space in your auditory environment as a way of creating silence in your thought process. Many of us are surrounded by some kind of aural stimulation all day long, so simply taking five minutes a day to turn off the TV, the radio, the phone, the computer and your mouth can go a long way to developing your ability to keep your own counsel out in the world with other people.

We are so conditioned to fill any silence with sound, that the impulse to do so can actually hinder our ability to protect our sacred selves with privacy. The discomfort we experience with silence can compel us to respond to things when we have no desire to do so, simply to fill the silence. By becoming comfortable with silence, both alone and when you are with others, you will strengthen your ability to be comfortable with it during those times when it would be best if you simply kept your own counsel.

One who has become comfortable with silence is perceived by others to be calm, deliberate, and centered. When you demonstrate these qualities, you will find that others rarely engage with you in any way that would threaten the privacy that you've worked so hard to cultivate. This is another manifestation of your profound privacy.

Conscious Sharing

One aspect of cultivating privacy is knowing what to share, when to share and how to share. Few (if any) of us live in isolation. As much as we might prefer and even be able to insert silence and privacy into our daily routines, we will still be required to engage with those that share our lives. They might be family, friends, employers, or even those we come in contact with casually throughout the day.

Given that our spiritual pursuits will make up more and more of our lives as we progress, how can we identify when to share, what to share and how to share it?

The first consideration, as we've already touched upon, is the relative newness of an idea or concept. The more recently we've begun to engage with a concept, the less appropriate it will be to share it with others. Most of the work that you will be doing will be exploratory at this stage, and nothing can dampen the spirit of exploration more than criticism and doubt. So if you have a relatively new idea that you've been drawn to explore, give it some time to settle in and take root. Don't be in such a hurry to get it out there.

Conversely, if you have been working with something for an extended period of time, and you find yourself developing a more extensive line of questioning around the concept, or you find yourself seeking a deeper understanding of it, you may do well to begin to open the idea up for consideration with other like-minded, like-hearted individuals.

You will need to rely upon your intuition in this area and guidance from your Sovereign Soul. There will be many opportunities to share with people who may not be your best resources for depth exploration, and both your gut and your Soul can help you identify and avoid them. When an idea reaches the stage where you feel ready to expose it to other elements and influences, use two basic tools to protect yourself and the idea: first, be really clear with yourself about the nature of the feedback you are seeking. Ask yourself, and your Sovereign Soul exactly what you hope to discover by opening the concept up to discussion with others.

Sometimes all you want is enrichment. You want to deepen your understanding of something by speaking to others who have approached the same or similar subjects from a different vantage point. Other times you might simply want reinforcement. This is a fine goal too – you may want to connect with other people whose experiences have been similar to your own, so that you can properly place your own experience within the framework of human experience overall. Many times just reading about others who have worked in similar areas and their experiences with the concept will be enough to meet this need.

For example, if you are working on the concept of fasting, the trajectory might look like this: Initially you mention to no one that you are contemplating fasting or experimenting with it. Eventually, you may want to explore different ways to fast, besides the obvious one related to food intake. So in this case you may want to connect with people who have worked with fasting on other levels, such as word fasting, or television fasting, or celibacy, for example. Or you may want to connect with others who have also experimented with fasting as it relates to food intake. In that case, you might read books or blogs related specifically to the experience of fasting with food.

You can see how you might tailor your own approach depending upon your purpose in sharing your explorations. At this point your sharing of your spiritual exploration does not become a general random feature of your interaction with others. You can carefully and deliberately determine first what you hope to gain by sharing, and then select the forum in which to most appropriately and supportively do that.

Determine Your Intention

So, how can you best determine your intention? Why do you seek to engage in this exchange? The driver behind the exchange will determine the nature of the exchange itself. If your goal is to manipulate or control the other person or persons in any way, then the exchange will necessarily become toxic. This is a very important aspect of communication and it can get tricky, because many times, particularly around spiritual topics, the sensation for the communicator is that of wanting to be of service, to help the other person.

However, if your help includes a requirement that they reach the same conclusions that you have, or that they modify their behavior somehow based upon your revelation, than you have initiated what will most often become a toxic exchange. It is one thing to give someone a gift. It is another thing entirely to give them a gift and then follow them around to see what they do with it to ensure that they get the proper amount of use or enjoyment out of it. Before you open your mouth, give some attention to your intention. Ask yourself truthfully whether communicating this information comes with any agenda whatsoever, and if so, what is that agenda?

Another thing to consider before you share your ideas, is to gauge as much as possible the intentions of the other people with whom you are about to communicate. This can be difficult to do because people's intentions are often hidden, sometimes by accident, but more often by choice. The key strategy is to allow enough space (and time) in the interaction for you to be able to distinguish between what you want out of the dynamic and what they want.

You can do this by just taking a breath, and allowing that question to rest in your mind before answering the other person's question. Sometimes that is all it takes to get the lay of the land. Once you've cleared your own agenda off the screen, (i.e. "I want this person to like me." "I want this person to hire me." "I want this person to leave me alone." "I want this person to see me as their equal." "I don't want this person to know other things about me." etc.) then you will have a better chance of reading their agenda (i.e. "This person wants me to be impressed." "This person wants me to like them." "This person wants to feel included." "This person is bored and is looking for entertainment" "This person is lonely, spiritually, and wants to connect." etc.)

Becoming more sensitive both to your agenda and to the agendas of others will support you in creating safe, healing spaces in which to share your spiritual journey so that both parties to the communication will be enriched by the exchange.

Privacy and Confrontation

What do you do, though, when you are confronted by a person whose agenda seems confrontational, and who is confronting you directly about some aspect of your journey? This sounds pretty dramatic, but in truth it happens all the time, sometimes in very small ways that we almost don't register as confrontational.

People get bored easily and may engage with you in a confrontational manner either to simply relieve that boredom, or to draw attention to themselves. They may persist in asking you direct, challenging and personal questions. They may employ sarcasm or a dismissive tone with you in order to stimulate you to engage at the very least by defending yourself. How can you maintain your profound privacy in this setting without either engaging in the confrontation, or enflaming it by dismissing it outright?

Silence is your friend here, again. Just taking a beat or two before you respond will allow you to identify the objective of the individual or group with whom you are potentially about to engage on a spiritual level. Once you ascertain that their intention is not one that serves either of you, it is a relatively simple matter to simply extricate yourself from the exchange with that alone.

Before you find yourself in that situation, try out a few "escape hatches" as I like to call them. Do your best to find a few statements that neither diminish the other person, nor commit you to any further discussion on the matter. Be aware that as satisfying as it might seem to dismiss them with some statement that indicates their "unworthiness" to engage with you on that level, this will probably only engage them further. You will have set yourself up as the unattainable, irresistible dynamic, and their reflex will be to continue to try and engage you relentlessly. If you truly seek to respect yourself and your journey, you will have to try and find one or two statements that neither insult nor dismiss the other person, while closing the conversation definitively.

Here are some suggested responses you might try:

> ‹ॐ "That's an interesting discussion, but probably not suited for this occasion. Perhaps another time."

- ෬ "I'd rather not talk about that right now, but what I would like to hear about is (insert some neutral topic related to the other person here)..."

- ෬ "Well, that's certainly a big conversation! It's unfortunate that I don't have time to give it the response it deserves! But tell me....(again, insert some topic that shifts the conversation away from spiritual matters.)"

I want to be clear that you will probably have to have several statements at the ready. For the most part, these spiritual "Looky-Loos" are persistent, and if you are being at all diplomatic or subtle in your response, they will probably keep picking at the lock for a while before they realize that the door is closed to them.

Practice Privacy

I want to encourage you to actually practice these statements out loud until they feel natural to you. As rehearsed as that seems, being provoked on a matter about which you feel protective and emotional can create an almost irresistible temptation to engage and defend. Even when you recognize that you are being deliberately baited by someone who clearly has no interest in sharing your views, but would rather suck some energy out of you by drawing you into a debate, you *will still find yourself tempted to engage*. That is just human nature.

Prepare yourself lovingly and with respect for both your human nature and for theirs. The more prepared you are to diffuse the situation, the more effective you will be. There is a reason that the old adage advises people in polite conversation never to engage in discussions centered on either politics or religion. In both topics, most people find themselves passionate in their responses, and often blindly so. When you understand the energetic violence of such an exchange and you recognize your budding spiritual illumination for the precious and tender thing that it is, you will never again expose it to such a volley of aggressive energy.

Instead, you will learn to safeguard it, leading it safely "out of the room" as if it were a small child, rather than exposing it to disrespect and outright attack. So take the time now to practice neutral, non-defensive responses to any toxic challenges on the spiritual front. You will be very happy to have them when the time comes, and it will. It always does.

Communicating in Safe Environments

Once you have established that the person with whom you are communicating is an open, receptive person whose agenda is not harmful to you, it will be important to look at the environment itself. Two key determinations will need to be made when discussing matters of a spiritual nature. The first is privacy on a very basic level. Even if you have determined that the individual or group with whom you are speaking is a safe space, is the room or location a private one?

Just as you would probably not spout off about the intimate details of your sexual life in a public space, it would not be appropriate to spout off about the intimate details of your spiritual life publicly either. So unless you are in a private location, where you feel reasonably secure about not being overheard or interrupted, refrain from discussing any spiritual matters that you regard as personal or private.

The second major consideration is time. It can be unpleasant and dissatisfying to share spiritual intimacies only to find that that time constraints did not allow either for full expression, or for the other person to respond in any way. You can avoid this by simply asking the other person or people *before you begin* if there is enough time to go into it.

The question sets the tone; it indicates that what you are about to share you consider worthy of sharing, and requiring of time and attention in order to be shared properly. If there is not enough time to share on that level, or if your listeners indicate that they are not willing/able to share on that level, then simply close the discourse politely and shift to a less personal topic. The key is to remind yourself always that what you are discussing is not a superficial topic by treating it as a topic with a certain amount of depth. When you begin to treat it with respect, so will others.

Note: Don't take it personally when you find yourself in a situation where a person is either unwilling or unable to connect with you respectfully and deeply on a spiritual subject. The capacity of any one person to engage with you on a depth level is just that, an indication of *their* capacity. It is not an indication of your worthiness or the worthiness of what you are sharing. People are able and willing to engage at various levels of depth and superficiality. Unless you can hold that in mind, you may find it frustrating when trying to communicate on spiritual matters. Simply put, if you find a teaspoon waiting for you, it is foolish to keep trying to empty your gallon jug into it. Better to simply move on, until you find a reservoir suitable for the quality and quantity of what you have to share.

Privacy and Our Intimates

One of the most challenging situations in which to maintain privacy around spiritual matters is when we are confronted by those with whom we are most intimate; the people we live with. Spiritual practice, particularly when it becomes a focal point in your life, can be very threatening to those with whom you live closely because it can change the way that you do everything. On a deeper level, as we connect with the Divine, the people whom we love the most may become afraid that our spiritual devotion might supersede or even nullify the love we have for them.

Every love that we share and express is an aspect of Divine Love. In some ways it's as if you've been receiving allotments of spring water from a messenger every day, and then, one day, you excitedly tell the messenger that you have begun to go directly to the spring itself. At first glance, you can see how threatening this would be to the spring-water bearer. But if you allow the story to play out a little further, you and the water bearer will see how much more wonderful it is for you both to journey to and from the spring together, sharing water and sharing the journey, neither of you dependent upon the other, and both fully nourished by the pure water.

So the fear that going to the Source will diminish the connection between you and your loved one was simply a mistaken assumption. Yet the assumption is usually made unconsciously, before the people involved have a chance to see it for what it is. It's a knee-jerk reflex, and at first it can be difficult for your "water bearers" to hear that you are now making the journey on your own, with or without them.

So how do you handle it when the profound privacy becomes difficult to maintain in your intimate relationships? What do you do when your loved ones feel left out or abandoned? What do you do when they challenge you directly about your explorations and realizations? How can you communicate your experience in a way that protects you from a potentially toxic exchange?

In a social setting with a non-intimate, you can simply extricate yourself from the situation. But your intimate companions, the people with whom you share your life, deserve some sort of communication about the shifts you are exploring and the changes you are experiencing in your inner dynamics.

The truth is that these people are also the ones who have the most at stake and the most power to create toxic exchanges for you, if the communication goes awry. They are the ones who can discourage and dissuade you more than any other people on the planet, simply because you love them, you respect them and you need them. They are your companions in life. They are your tribe. Naturally you would be afraid to disappoint or alienate them. So, how can you include them in your spiritual life without laying yourself wide open to any toxic aspects of the exchange? How can you protect yourself and still honor and include them?

Healthy Boundaries

The key in this situation is healthy boundaries; both setting them and holding them. In this task, preparation will be your best friend. There will be many areas of your spiritual practice that are readily available to your loved ones, but there will also be things about it that you will feel the need to keep private. You will know what those things are if you take the time to contemplate them in that light. Making those distinctions, and then being willing to stand up for them will be an important part of your process.

Know from the outset that having some sort of balance between what you are and are not willing or able to share will be very helpful to you in strengthening the existing intimacy between you and your loved ones, while maintaining your privacy with the Divine. But balance cannot be achieved without making distinctions, and it takes heart and courage to make them. So, while it may be easier to completely exclude or completely include the people in your life, you must make time to discern what you are able to share and with whom. And you must find a way to enforce those distinctions without insulting your loved ones. Additional resources to support you in making those distinctions are available in the Sovereign Soul Sanctuary online community at www.sovereignsoul.org.

It is an easy way out and a trap to pull the "superiority" card on people when you are fearful of defending your boundaries. Know that there is another way, and that it too will be discovered and become natural if you give yourself the time and the opportunity to discover it. There is a way of enforcing boundaries that diminishes the other person and there is another, better way that respects and inspires them. Find the latter way, and it will be a lot easier to employ than the former.

The important thing to remember when determining and maintaining boundaries with those who are closest to you is that the more you can be clear about intentions (yours and theirs), the more easily you will be able to navigate your own boundaries without either betraying your own trust or diminishing your connections with others.

Respect (for yourself and others) is not only key to this process; it is a profound practice in and of itself. You will become more and more familiar with the sensation of self respect and respect for others as you journey further and further along your spiritual path.

Chapter Five
Creating a Consistent Spiritual Practice

Now that you've begun to prepare space mentally and physically to welcome your Sovereign Soul, created structures to protect your privacy and learned how to listen for guidance by following the resonance within your environment, it is time to look seriously at the elements of a consistent spiritual practice.

A successful and reliable spiritual practice will have four qualities apparent in each aspect: Consistency, Creativity, Connection, and Commitment. The more you can implement the four C's into each element of your practice, the more successful you will be and the more the practice will be able to serve you and your development as a spiritual being. We've touched on each of them at various points so far, but they deserve a little more of our attention as we begin to put the elements of the spiritual practice into place.

Consistency

Any reliable spiritual practice will demonstrate a level of consistency in its implementation. For much of this work it will be the quality of what you are doing rather than the quantity that will make the difference. If you can take one small element of your spiritual practice and practice it consistently, you will begin to find it more and more enriching as you go. Repetition, and the cultivation of self-discipline around soulful habits is fundamental to being able to rely upon those habits under times of stress or in crisis. Under duress, we go back to what we know. In order for your spiritual practice to be immediately available to you when you need it most, you need to reinforce it with your consistent application of the elements that form the practice. So doing one small thing well and often is preferable to doing many things superficially and sporadically. As an independent seeker you must allow yourself to develop within the practice, and that means learning to count on it and grow with it through repetition. It is your consistency that makes your practice trustworthy.

Creativity

Another foundational quality to a successful spiritual practice is the application of creativity to the entire practice. Your creativity is the unique connection that you have with the elements of the practice. It is the unique way in which you engage here and now with elements that have been part of spiritual practice for centuries. When it comes to spiritual practice, there really isn't anything new happening anywhere. No matter how new it seems to you, each aspect of spirituality has been implemented across cultures and across generations since the beginning of man's search for spiritual fulfillment.

Your creative approach to the practice is what makes it unique. It gives significance to what you are doing, and allows you to engage with an ancient ritual in a brand new way by being completely present. Your creativity takes the "science" of faith and transforms it into an art. As you apply your unique approach to each of the elements, as you bring your unique self to the practice, so the practice becomes your offering to the Divine within you and to Divinity as a whole. Your practice becomes your contribution to the spiritual growth of all beings, and allows you to participate fully in the experience, giving as much as you receive. Your creativity is what makes your practice beautiful.

Connection

Connection speaks to the relationships between you, your practice, your Sovereign Soul and the world at large. Your practice cannot exist in a vacuum and thrive. Everything that you do within your practice, each element that you put in place, relates to everything else, and it is the existence of those relationships that will bring meaning to your path. Those relationships exist whether or not you are aware of them, but your conscious awareness and acknowledgement of them can elevate your practice energetically, and strengthen the relationships themselves.

What you are bringing when you bring connection is a willingness to witness the interrelatedness of not just the elements of your practice, but of yourself and of your Sovereign Soul in your life. You begin to see your place in the universe as you allow yourself to become conscious of the connections between your practice and your life, yourself and your Soul, your Soul and Source, Source and all beings, etc. This web of interconnectivity and support will allow you to deepen and enlighten your own path within it. The connections that you are willing to experience are what will make your practice meaningful.

Commitment

Commitment is your willingness and ability to follow through and complete things. It is what allows you to trust yourself to keep your word, and to stand in the center of your integrity as a spiritual being. Over and over in the physical world you will be given opportunities to test the strength of your resolve and to establish faith in yourself. Some of these opportunities you will recognize immediately, others will take a while to become apparent, and still others you will miss entirely and find yourself falling back upon diminishing habits. You are falling in love with your Soul, and as with any process of falling in love, you will find that love tested – not because you are not worthy of it, but because you are developing spiritually, and development requires expansion. As you expand, you will be given greater and greater opportunities to continue to expand, to fortify your resolve and deepen your willingness to engage.

Your commitment to staying the course, seeking the expansion, surrendering what needs surrendering, working with what shows up, abandoning resistance whenever possible, and making your faith your priority will be the key to your progress as a spiritual being. Your commitment is essential and incredibly fulfilling once you begin to realize it. When you follow through, finish what you start, and embrace what comes your way, then you become most able to benefit from your Soul's guidance, and to benefit others as well. This makes you a blessing to the world. It is your commitment to your practice that makes it powerful.

Now that we've examined the core qualities that support a successful and satisfying spiritual practice, it is time to look at the various elements that you can incorporate into that practice. I use the term "incorporate" very specifically – meaning *to form the body of the practice*. Each of these elements can support and enrich the others, when you give them physical expression, when you embody them, as it were. Each one, working with the others, will form the foundation of your practice – they will be the bones upon which you will flesh out your growth. But also, and equally importantly, each one can be a portal, an opportunity for you to receive guidance from your Sovereign Soul.

To begin with, you may want to read through the rest of the chapter entirely before selecting one or two ways to begin working with these elements. As you read, just let the ideas wash over you and see what resonates. Your beautiful Sovereign Soul will make clear to you where to begin. Rather than approaching this in a linear fashion, allow your intuition to take over, and feel your way. What feels like a good place to start probably is!

Creating an Altar

An altar can serve several functions to the seeker. It can be a place to make offerings to Divinity as you understand it, it can be a place to set intentions, it can be a place where you make requests, and it can be a place where you celebrate your gratitude. It can even be all of these things simultaneously. I like to think of my altar as sort of a postal box between myself and my Sovereign Soul. It is a place where I can leave messages, via symbols, images and offerings, to my Soul. It is an art form as well, allowing me to bring the creative force of my love for my Soul into manifestation – so I decorate my altar lovingly, beautifully, to express my gratitude for her constant loving presence in my life.

Your altar can also serve as a reminder to you to stay focused on your path. Each time you approach, or even see your altar, it brings your purpose and your faith powerfully into your mind. If you are in an environment where it feels right to do so, it may be helpful to put your altar in a prominent place in your living space – somewhere where you can see it often, and where it is always in your thoughts.

Tending the altar, keeping it clean and fresh and beautiful is a nurturing, tender way to express your consistency and to demonstrate your willingness to be of service in life. Opportunities to express this sentiment can be few and far between for most of us in modern life, so you may find this deeply satisfying as you become better and better at it. Tending the altar can become a meditation in and of itself, if you bring your full attention to it while you do it, and do it with reverence and devotion.

To begin with, it will be helpful for you to ask your Sovereign Soul for guidance on creating an altar that will be most useful and significant to you. You can do that either as you journal or sitting in quiet meditation. Some questions you may want to pose might include the following:

 C3 Where would be best to place my altar?

C3 What intentions would be best to bring to my altar?

C3 What could make my altar even more meaningful and powerful?

C3 What natural elements would be appropriate for my altar?

C3 What images or symbols would be helpful to include?

C3 What deities, ascended masters or guides would be helpful to represent there?

cs What offerings would be meaningful for me?

cs What would be the most meaningful ways for me to use the altar?

Of course, these are just a few questions you might pose to your Sovereign Soul. You will certainly have others as you work with your altar. If you approach your altar with consistency, decorate it with creativity, allow it to connect you with the Divine, and commit to keeping it fresh, current and beautiful, you will find the practice intensely gratifying.

There are many good books about how to build an altar, different approaches to working with altars and what sorts of things you can include as you develop your altar. For additional inspiration, you can find more resources in the Sovereign Soul Sanctuary online community at www.sovereignsoul.org.

Developing a Library

One of the most powerful and useful tools for the independent mystic is a well-stocked spiritual library. The contents of your library will become invaluable to your spiritual growth and to developing your connection with your Sovereign Soul. Though most of us associate the act of reading with the intellect, mystics throughout history (since the written word was invented) have traditionally engaged in the spiritual practice of "contemplative reading."

Contemplative reading is sort of a cross between reading and meditating. It is the act of meditating upon the text as you are reading it. In this way, the spiritual text becomes a journey rather than a destination, and the experience of reading it becomes the path. This activity is a really important component of the independent seeker's practice, because without that level of attention and focus, she may find herself with only a superficial understanding of the multitude of spiritual teachings to which she is exposed.

Think of it this way – seekers within the framework of an organized religion will spend years poring over a single spiritual text until the deeper meanings have a chance to sift down into their consciousness. But because the independent seeker is exposed to so many different spiritual texts, she can find herself jumping from one approach to another, without giving any one of them a chance to take root and reveal its deeper significance. Contemplative reading is an opportunity for you to slow down and steep yourself in the wisdom of the text. It is an opportunity for you to let it soak into you, and then overflow into the rest of your practice, informing each of the other elements as you go. If you practice this *consistently*, allow yourself to see how what you are reading *connects* to other elements in your practice, approach those connections *creatively* and *commit* to following through until you finish the text, you will make yourself available to the teaching on every level and allow it to fully impact you. You can find more information on the practice of contemplative reading in the Sovereign Soul Sanctuary online community at www.sovereignsoul.org.

One of the first steps to building an effective library is to take stock of what you already have and collect all your resources in one place. Think about how you want to organize them so that you can easily find what you are looking for. You can do it alphabetically, but I have found it very helpful to organize around topic rather than by title or author's name. This makes things much easier to find if you can't quite think of the name of the book, or if you have a craving to explore a specific topic but are not sure which resource to start with. Give your books on spiritual topics their own space, distinct from the rest of your books. Don't limit your library to books alone, though, but include music, audio programs and DVDs as well.

As you begin to collect additional resources in your library, think in terms of practical application – you can use the table of contents of this book to inspire general areas for research, if that helps. Do your best to include a variety of approaches and modalities in your library, as well as some of the basic spiritual texts of the major wisdom traditions. You may also find it helpful to invest in several reference-style books on spirituality that provide a little bit of information about each of the major traditions. These can be a valuable resource for you when you seek to expand into a new area.

Once you have assembled your resources, review the contents of your library to determine if any particular modality that is missing – you want to make sure that all avenues are open to you so try to make sure to have some materials that approach you on a visual level (images, art, symbols, use of color, etc.), on an auditory level (music, sound/tone, audio programs, chanting, books on tape, etc.) and on a physical level (use of physical space, body movement, Feng Shui, etc.). In this way you will have resources available to you that allow your Sovereign Soul to reach you on every level.

Having a substantial spiritual library, with both breadth and depth of subject matter, is vital to your growth and offers you many opportunities to experience each of the four C's as you work your way through it. You can find more information and resources to support you in building a comprehensive spiritual library in the Sovereign Soul Sanctuary online community at www.sovereignsoul.org.

Explorative Journaling

Journaling will be one of the most profound elements of your practice as you travel the path to spiritual development. Your journal not only creates a record of the events and insights that you are experiencing, but it creates a context for them. Your journal offers a safe space to explore your options and allows you to experience your journey authentically and honestly, holding nothing back. It functions as a means of communicating with your Sovereign Soul – a place where you can write letters to her and do dialoguing exercises that allow her to offer you insights.

If you have never dialogued with your Soul in writing, it is a fairly simple exercise. You begin by writing your question with your dominant hand, and then write your response with your non-dominant hand. Try to remain as open and receptive as you can. Sometimes it helps to begin this exercise with a written prayer, asking for guidance and assistance. If you become familiar with the voice of your Soul as distinct from your own, you may find it easier to simply write both sides of the conversation with your dominant hand for the sake of expediency, but to begin with, try it with both hands, allowing yourself time to open up and receive the guidance you've asked for.

Journaling is also a wonderful way to work with your dreams, which we will explore in more depth later in this chapter. For now, it is enough to know that recording your dreams alongside your prayers and your insights deepens the connection between all three, and allows an energetic exchange to happen, whereby each informs the others.

Journaling gives you the space and the time to explore your options when you are stuck, or find yourself at a fork in the road. Sometimes it can be helpful just to write out, in detail, the opportunities that are being presented to you, and see what comes of it. Things often become much more clear when seen in writing on the printed page. You also have an opportunity to look at the quality of your handwriting in each of the options, to see if there are any differences in the quality of your responses.

Your handwriting can offer you tremendous insight into how you actually feel about something that you may not be able to register when you just think the thoughts instead of writing them down. You may want to review your journal entries with handwriting analysis in mind, and see if you can pick out any characteristic differences between entries depending upon the topics. Some topics will appear flowing, relaxed and open, while the writing on other topics may be cramped, erratic, or tense. This gives you a wonderful opportunity to "see" your thoughts, possibly for the first time.

Another wonderful use for your journal is to record quotes and insights that you are finding in different texts. This is especially useful if you are like me and you read several books at the same time. Being able to assemble the insights and revelations into one text (your journal) side by side, gives you a completely different understanding of what they mean and how they interrelate. It also creates a wonderful context for some of the other entries – for example, if you have recorded a dream, and then a few pages later you have added a quote, you may see, when you look back, how the quote commented on the dream, or how the dream anticipated the quote. This interplay between various resources and points of inspiration provides a vital opportunity for you to open the communication between yourself and your Sovereign Soul. You may not know how they all fit together as they happen, but when you bring them together in your journal, you can suddenly see the pattern – the significance. The more you do it, the more you will begin to recognize the influence of your Soul on all aspects of your life.

Journaling absolutely benefits from the four C's – its value will be enhanced by your *consistency* in showing up to the page, your *creativity* in applying a variety of approaches to journaling, your ability to recognize the *connections* between entries, and your *commitment* to acting on the insights you receive.

Prayer

Prayer is a powerful and humbling part of every spiritual seeker's path. There are as many ways to pray as there are paths, but there are a few basic models which may be helpful to start with.

Structured Prayer

Some faiths have built powerful rituals into their prayer structures, including where you pray, when you pray, what you wear, which way you face, how you hold your body, and what you say. Although this may seem restrictive to you as an independent seeker, it is useful to acknowledge the value in this model, so that you might feel free to experiment with it yourself.

A structured prayer model allows for great *consistency* for the seeker, letting the prayer sink in really deeply through repetition. It also makes it very simple for the seeker to participate – you don't have to think about what you want to say, or how you mean to pray – you just do it, as prescribed. This frees you up to feel the prayer, since you've disconnected the intellectual reasoning that may have gone into thinking up your prayer and can allow yourself to simply sink into the words.

Also, the fact that so much ritual is surrounding this style of prayer allows you to engage with the prayer on all levels – physically, visually and on an auditory level – you are engaging all systems in the practice, and that can yield powerful results. It can literally change your mind and your state immediately because the pattern is so beautifully etched in your experience. The other thing this style can do for you is to strengthen your spiritual discipline. Spiritual discipline is an essential ingredient to expansion, and a simple prayer, said in the same way at the same time every day can really support your ability to fortify that discipline. Once fortified, you will have it available to you for other things, and in other ways when you need it.

Blessings

Blessings could also be considered relatively structured prayers, in that they usually have a simple, fairly standardized format – but the difference is that you can say them anywhere, at any time, for anything. The value to this model is a gradual sifting of your spiritual life into your "non-spiritual" life over time. The more you can bless things, the more you can bring your attention back to your spiritual life in the midst of your regular life. Each time you do it, you create an opportunity for your Soul to touch you, to move you.

Blessings feel really good, too. They create a sensation of well-being in your heart and mind as you speak them (or think them), and they re-affirm your constant connection to the Source of all blessings, in everything, all the time. The more you bless things, the more you begin to look for things to bless, so even the spaces in between your blessings are imbued with an attention to Spirit, and a willingness to participate in the highest good for all concerned. This awareness serves to deepen your *connection* to the Divine.

Experiment a little with blessing, and see how different you feel after even one day of consciously blessing everything you touch. Bless your food, bless your drink, bless your activities, bless your home, your vehicle, your workplace, bless your body, bless your activities, bless your resources, bless the people around you, bless your animals, bless all of nature, bless other drivers on the road – look for an opportunity to bless at every moment, and see how it feels to engage with prayer in this way. I think you will be surprised at what a difference you feel almost immediately.

Prayers of Gratitude

I don't think it is possible to exaggerate the impact that prayers of gratitude will have on your spiritual practice. Like blessings, prayers of gratitude feel really, really good while you are praying them. Even if you start out praying your gratitude from a less than positive position, by the end you will almost always have uplifted your energy and opened your heart.

Gratitude is an open, expansive, flowing, joyful state, and the more you can express that to your Soul and to Source, the more available you become spiritually. There is no "right" way to do this – except often. Do it often. Combine it with your prayers of blessing if that helps. Pray it out loud if you can. Take the time whenever possible to revel in the bounty of blessings that make up your life. Challenge yourself to discover the wonder in the simplest of things – here is an opportunity to let your *creativity* shine – you can express gratitude for the breath that you just took, gratitude for a parking spot, gratitude for a pause in a conversation that gives you a minute to collect your thoughts. See how simple you can make it.

Later, when you are in the habit of praying your gratitude, you will begin to find opportunities to pray gratitude for things that maybe you didn't feel so grateful for initially – things that didn't go the way you planned, or that frightened or hurt you. When you get to the place where you can genuinely be grateful for all of the events in your life – when you begin to see the merit in even the things you would not have wished for, and you can offer your thanks for those things, then you will have developed the ability to offer non-resistance, and you will be that much closer to letting your Sovereign Soul direct your life completely. Every time you meet that opportunity with your gratitude, you align yourself more fully with the most beautiful and trustworthy plan for your life – the one your Sovereign Soul has designed for you, for your highest good and the good of all concerned. Practice gratitude at every opportunity and watch your spiritual practice expand in response. Gratitude is huge.

Prayers for Guidance

Praying for guidance is an extremely useful and easy way to incorporate prayer into your daily life. Pretty much everything you do would benefit from a little help and guidance. These prayers, like blessings and gratitude, can be very, very simple – just ask for help. Ask for help with everything. Spirit loves to assist you in whatever way you will let it. So ask for help, and then take a moment to receive it. The asking part is the expressive component of this prayer, but the receptive part is the most important bit. Take a moment to clear your thoughts and feelings and just remain open to what comes. Your guidance can show up in a variety of ways – an insight, a feeling, a physical sensation, or even an event that will show up after you ask for help. So try to stay as open and receptive as possible when you are waiting for the guidance. Many people get so caught up in the asking part that they forget to wait for the answer. Allow both aspects of this prayer to happen in order for it to be most useful. Allow the circuit to be completed.

Prayers for Intercession

Intercession is different from guidance in that you are actually asking for Divine Intervention on your behalf. When you pray for guidance, you are usually asking for help with what to do. When you pray for intercession, you are literally turning it over to the Divine. You are releasing your control of the outcome, or even the need to know what the highest outcome will be. You are putting all of that directly into God's hands on your behalf. These prayers are simple prayers as well, but can be incredibly powerful because they serve to acknowledge and reinforce your role and the role of the Divine in the events of your life. There is a lot that your Soul can do on your behalf, if you let her, but you have to be willing to ask, you have to be willing to trust and you have to be willing to turn it over. That's where your *commitment* comes in.

Some seekers will wait until a crisis, something that they feel they cannot handle themselves, before they are willing to surrender control and turn it over to God. This is often because they believe they should not call on the Divine if they think they can handle it themselves. But God loves to help you. Your Soul loves to help you at every opportunity. The more you turn over to Spirit, the more you will be able to serve the highest good for all concerned and the more you will be able align yourself with your own highest good. It is far more effective to get used to turning events and situations over to God as often as you can, well in advance of a crisis, than it is to only call for help as a last resort. You don't have to wait until you are out of options to hand it over to the Divine – you can surrender to the highest good at any point along the way. Your prayer can be as simple as this "God, please intervene in this situation on my behalf and for the highest good of all concerned." Then, turn it over. Literally hand it over. And trust.

Prayers for Specific Things

Praying for specific things can get tricky – don't let yourself get caught up in value judgments around what you can and can't pray for. The truth is that you can pray for anything you want to pray for. The trick is that you have to remember that you are not just shouting into the void. Your prayers are being heard and received. If you are praying for something that is not aligned with your highest good or the good of all concerned then you will probably feel it, even while you are praying. There are no "right" and "wrong" things to pray for – there are simply those things that are aligned with your spiritual development and those that are not. If you are praying for a pound of cocaine so you can sell it to school children, for example, the answer to your prayer will probably be very different than if you are praying for the health and well-being of a dear friend. The energetic contribution that you make with your prayer, will be met by an infinitely appropriate response from the Divine. As your bond with your Sovereign Soul begins to deepen, the response will become more and more immediately discernable. When you practice praying for specific things there are a few tips to make those prayers more satisfying, meaningful and useful to your development as a spiritual being.

Always qualify your prayers with "if it is in the highest good for all concerned" no matter what you are praying for. This is shorthand for turning it over to Divine discernment, and acknowledging that you are not in a position to know the full ramifications of your request. Also try to make your requests in terms of the feeling states that the thing will bring you. You can be as specific as you want in your request, but be sure to include the state you want to experience along with it – for example, if I want to pray for that new job, I would pray for it, but I would also say "...so that I might feel fulfilled, respected, creative and financially secure in my livelihood..." after my specific request. This way I am really communicating the essence of my prayer – it is these feeling states that I am really requesting, and the Divine will intervene on my behalf if the job I am asking for would not create those states in me, were I to get what I was asking for. It is also helpful to include the words "This or something better" somewhere in a specific prayer request, so that Spirit can bring you the best possible solution to your request. We are often trapped by our limited thinking, and we do not ask for what we would truly want because we hadn't considered that there might be anything better than what we were already asking for.

If you approach prayer requests with these caveats in mind, you eliminate many of the barriers that stand between you and your Soul's ability to provide for you. If you do it with respect, humility and gratitude, you can feel free to come to your Soul with anything you hope for, and expect the best possible answer, even when the best possible answer is "No," as it sometimes is.

Prayers for Comfort

These are some of your most powerful prayers, and yet they are often neglected. We just forget about them, especially when we are in need of comfort. I want to remind you that your Soul wants you to show up exactly as you are. Even when you are a mess. Even when you have lost your faith. Even when you are consumed with anger. Show up. Ask for comfort. Ask for peace. Ask for help. Your Sovereign Soul, the highest, most beautiful and compassionate aspect of your being, is there specifically to intercede on your behalf – and to remind you that you are one with the Source of all comfort, of all peace. Your Soul's mission is to be there for you when you most need her. Do not wait until you "feel like it" to ask for her help. When you are being what feels like the worst version of you, turn immediately to the best part of you and ask for her presence, ask for her help. You know when you need it. Don't be afraid to ask for it. Ask early and ask often. You cannot wear her out and she will never let you down.

The Nature of Prayer

Now that you've reviewed some basic structures of prayer to include in your practice, you may want to ask for some guidance around when and how to implement them. Today take some time to think about the nature of prayer. You may want to journal a little on it, using the questions below to stimulate your exploration:

- ✂ How am I already praying in my life?

- ✂ When do I usually pray?

- ✂ What is my most familiar style of prayer?

- ✂ How can I expand my experience of prayer?

- ✂ Which types of prayers have I been neglecting?

- ✂ How can I best support myself to vary the role of prayer in my practice?

- ✂ How would my prayer life look if I were more consistent with it?

- ✂ How would my prayer life look if I were more creative with it?

- ✂ How would my prayer life look if I began to focus more on using it to connect?

- ✂ How would my prayer life look if I were more committed with it?

- ✂ Ask yourself what activities you already do with full awareness and gratitude.

Experiment with the insights you discover in this exploration. Allow the wisdom to trickle into you slowly. Trust that you have the answers you need and that you are ready to receive them. Allow what springs to mind to guide you in your responses to daily life, and record your experiences when you do.

In this way you can slowly allow more and more of the light of your Sovereign Soul to express itself, radiating through you, rippling out into all areas of your life. Remember, you don't pray because you are trying to fix the problems you think you have, but instead you pray to reveal the essential solution that you *are* and that you always have been.

Meditation

Almost all spiritual practice will involve some form of meditation because of the enormous spiritual benefits it can offer. As you did with prayer, you will find many forms of meditation from which to choose. You can experiment with all of them, or you can pick one to focus on exclusively. I won't delve too much into the many types of meditation because there are so many wonderful books and resources on the subject, but I will take a minute to outline the benefits and to describe a few of the more popular styles of meditation to get you started.

Meditation can offer you many rich rewards as you begin to include it in your regular practice. It can reveal the habits of your mind, it can create a sense of calm in the core of your being that stays with you all day, it can bring you into the present and it can allow you to release both the past and the future so that you can be here now. These are all profoundly impactful spiritual benefits that will support every other aspect of your practice.

Silent Meditation

Silent meditation is the style which you are probably most familiar with, and may have even tried before. This style can seem intimidating to the beginner, but yields tremendous results if you can allow yourself the time and the patience to stick with it. Even very short spans of silent meditation can prove to be surprisingly effective.

Chanting

Another popular form of meditation is chanting. Some advocate the use of a specific phrase or expression, while others find value in varying the chant depending upon circumstance or intention. There are some wonderful resources on the topic available, many including CD's with chants that you can follow. Chanting is a very grounding, centering style of meditation, and one which I would encourage you to explore. Ask for guidance about which chants would be most beneficial for you and how best to implement this form of meditation into your practice.

Walking Meditation

Walking or moving meditations are also extremely popular, particularly in the Buddhist tradition. This style asks you to complete some repetitive activity with great focus and concentration on the task, bringing your complete attention and awareness to what you are doing in the moment. One of the reasons this style is so popular is that it does not require that you sit still for long periods of time in silence. The focused attention (or mindfulness) that you bring to the activity becomes something you can tap into anytime, anywhere, while doing almost anything, so it's a great style to start with, since you can integrate it into some activities that you may already be doing.

Experiment with these and other forms of meditation to see what works and what is most appropriate for you at the present time. Remember that the *consistency* with which you enter into meditation, your *creativity* in finding styles that suit you, the ways in which you can *connect* it to other elements of your practice, and your *commitment* to stick with it even when you reach a plateau and get bored with it (as you will, from time to time!) will all determine how effective it can be for you, and how powerfully it can align you with your Sovereign Soul. Meditation is a portal, a bridge between your conscious, waking personality and the most enlightened, evolved aspects of your being. Use it.

Creativity and Art

Many seekers neglect to include an element of art and creativity in their spiritual practice because they don't see themselves as being visually "artistic" or inspired in that area. I would encourage you to experiment with this aspect of spiritual practice regardless of what you think about your skills. The truth is that your Sovereign Soul is extremely creative, and communicates a great deal of information to you through the use of symbols. This is the same part of you that sends you information via your dream images, so working with symbols and images in your artwork is no great stretch for her.

It doesn't matter if you doodle, finger paint, or make a collage; your Sovereign Soul can use your creativity to speak to you with symbol. Try to suspend your need to judge the product of your artistic explorations, and focus entirely upon the process. The colors, textures and images that you feel particularly drawn to, and the way they relate to one another visually in the space will be clues. You are looking for what you resonate with from moment to moment. Resonance is the language of your Soul. For many artists, seeking out and expressing that resonance has always been at the heart of their work, whether recognized or not, and their Sovereign Soul has been expressing herself in that way for years.

If you are already an artist, you may find it useful to work within whatever medium you are most comfortable, but don't neglect the opportunity to step outside of that medium. Sometimes the territory in which you have the least skill (control) is the one you will find most rewarding. It is in these places that you can turn over control to a higher part of yourself, and trust what develops to be an authentic communication from your Sovereign Soul, rather than your own intellectual effort. Your lack of experience and familiarity can create a "beginner's mind" which is naturally open and receptive. So allow yourself to experiment with a new form of artistic expression whenever possible.

If you do not already consider yourself an artist, then any medium you feel drawn to will be a chance to adopt the receptive stance of a beginner's mind. As an unskilled artist, you will be responding only to the resonance of the images and symbols themselves, and be less likely than an "artist" would be to let your desire for artistic perfection undermine the expression of your Soul.

No matter what your actual history is with art, allow yourself to enter the artistic arena as a novice, open to the experience and without any sense of judgment wherever possible. The only rule to follow is to consistently hold the explorative stance. This is the most useful and powerful approach to this work. Let neither your vast experience in this medium nor your complete ignorance of it stand in your way. You may want to explore painting, sketching, doodling, collage, sculpture, quilting, working with mandalas, and assemblage. The Sovereign Soul Sanctuary online community has additional resources available to support your exploration at www.sovereignsoul.org.

Working with Your Dreams

As you become more and more familiar with symbolic communications from your beloved Sovereign Soul, you may find yourself remembering more and more of your dreams. The act of working consciously with symbols during your normal waking hours may have the added effect of stimulating your conscious mind to remember more and more of the symbolic content of your subconscious life. This is a good sign! You have always had dreams, and they have always been a part of your spiritual life, but you may not have been ready to absorb or assimilate that content consciously, and so forgot them when you awoke. Your working with the language of symbols through art and creativity will signal to your conscious mind that you are ready for even more communications on that level.

The most important part of working with dreams is simply recording them. And to do that, you must become willing to prioritize it. It can be inconvenient to write down dreams immediately upon waking, but that's what's required. In a sense, working with your dreams is a discipline, like any other spiritual discipline, and you may need to commit to it before it becomes natural or inspired. You don't need to analyze your dreams right away - though you may find yourself doing that naturally - you just need to get them written down. Even if all you remember is the feeling of a dream, or the flavor of it, go ahead and record that. That's all you have to do. Your action will signal to your Sovereign Soul that you are committed and receptive to her communication via your dreams, and that you will pay attention and treat that communication with respect.

An extremely powerful style of working with your dreams is to approach them with a specific agenda. Ask your Sovereign Soul to communicate with you specifically around a series of ideas and questions, and then prepare yourself and be ready to record any responses that come to you through your dreams. Once you get in the habit of working with your dreams in this way, you will find it an incredibly powerful and prominent tool in your spiritual development. The Divine (and particularly your own Sovereign

Soul) loves to communicate with you in dreams because of the intense energetic charge they carry, and because so much can be communicated on so many levels. Complex information becomes simple and understandable when delivered symbolically.

Even when you do not consciously remember a dream, your psyche will have received the benefit of the information it contained. In the beginning, you may find that the only dreams that bubble to the surface of your conscious mind are the ones that you were not able to absorb and integrate subconsciously. In other words, you may only become aware of your problem areas. Any messages that were successfully received and integrated during the sleep cycle will not need to intrude consciously upon your waking mind.

However, when you specifically ask to become conscious of certain things, dreams related to those things will find their way into your conscious waking mind automatically, simply because you asked them to. You will find that not every dream remembered indicates an area that "needs attention." Sometimes you remember just because you requested that you would. The memory of these dreams can be interpreted as a signal that you are right on track with whatever you are doing.

Analyzing your dreams can be a rich and rewarding aspect of your spiritual life and much has been written to assist you in learning to decode the unique symbolic language of your Sovereign Soul in your dreams. As your explorations deepen, you will find that your ability to perceive and understand the symbolic aspects of your waking life becomes easier as well. You can find additional tools and resources to support your exploration of dreamwork, available in the Sovereign Soul Sanctuary online community at www.sovereignsoul.org.

Working with Sound and Music

One of the spiritual practices most under-rated and under-utilized by independent spiritual seekers is working with sound and music. Every organized faith has a worship element involving sound and/or music because it represents one of the most energetically stimulating ways to connect with the Divine. Sound and music consist of patterns of vibration which can bypass the conscious waking mind, and actually change the energetic body of the listener. Spiritual seekers since the beginning of history have been working with energy in this way and the tradition remains strong even in modern religion although they tend not to consciously acknowledge the energetic import of the worship song. But independent seekers very often forget to make this powerful practice a regular part of their spiritual lives – mostly because musical worship is usually done in groups, and independent seekers are very rarely assembled in groups.

To begin, you may want to take stock of your current sound and music library and pull out CD's and MP3's that are spiritually uplifting for a separate section of your Spiritual Library devoted to music and sound. Review your music collection and explore categorizing the music in terms of the energetic shift each piece represents. You can make yourself "mix tapes" (playlists) that shift energy in specific ways. For example some music is calming, some invigorating, some is comforting and some is inspirationally beautiful and uplifting. Creating playlists with different energetic flavors, and keeping them with you on an MP3 player is a great way to incorporate musical worship into your daily life. You can immediately change the energy in your body and connect your heart to the Divine simply by listening to a song or two. See if you can find ways to work spiritually charged music into your normal routine – during commutes, meals, exercise, or housekeeping. Whatever you do normally, try to consciously include spiritually uplifting music in the activity.

A next step might be to start to collect musical instruments, even simple ones, like a rattle, or a drum, and work them into your practice. Simple musical instruments can accompany your chanting or meditation, for example, or be used to clear energy before you begin a new endeavor. I keep a small cedar wood rattle in my car and use it to clear energy if I get tense in traffic, for example. Don't forget that your voice is a wonderful, simple instrument for you to work with in the beginning, and explore how you can use your voice musically to support your practice. When you sing, you actually create the vibrations with your vocal chords, rather than merely responding to them from external sources.

If you already play an instrument, try to approach it with a beginner's mind – again, allowing Spirit to inspire you, and really letting the music you are playing fill your mind, heart and body vibrationally. Even if you don't play the instrument, play *with* it – experiment with different tones, and how they feel in your body, and with different simple melodies. The relationships between different tones, and between the sound and the silence – the rhythms and the intervals – all have different vibrational value to your being, so any exploration you do with music will have an opening effect on you and allow your Sovereign Soul to better support you. You will probably find yourself drawn to certain sounds, rhythms and intervals, so just go with it. The idea is to create that opening, and work with music on a purely vibrational level if you can.

You may want to incorporate movement/dance into your work with music, so that you can allow your whole body to participate in the shift. This is a really lovely way to let music to take on a greater role in your spiritual practice. Start slow so that you will not overdo it, or injure yourself – even gentle, subtle movement to music can have a powerful impact on you, and create an energetic opening. Begin your movement and dance in private if possible so that you can allow yourself to be completely unselfconscious – experiencing the movement with the sound in a way that does not require thought or stimulate self-judgment. Later you may find it empowering to explore this aspect with other people, but in the beginning, just give yourself some privacy as you would with any other spiritual endeavor.

As you get more familiar with working with sound and music, begin to explore ways to do it with other like-minded and like-hearted people. There is tremendous power in experiencing inspirational music with others, even if they are not necessarily there for their own spiritual purposes. Remember, whether or not they know it, their energy is shifting. So being in a room full of others who are experiencing a vibrational shift that is in alignment with your own can be a very moving experience. You will find many opportunities available to do this once you begin to look for them; concerts, fairs, dances, and even classes, like a yoga class for example.

Spend some time journaling on how best to include sound and music as a consistent part of your spiritual practice and how you can ensure a variety of conscious experiences with music and sound as you move forward. Additional resources are available to support you in the Sovereign Soul Sanctuary online community at www.sovereignsoul.org.

Incorporating Physical Movement

Soulful movement is a way to celebrate the body's connection to the Divine and express that connection in a physical manner. Like music, this is another area that many independent seekers neglect in their spiritual practice. Often we may be involved in various activities involving movement, without looking at how a spiritual intention could change that movement, or strengthen our spiritual lives. Adding soulful physical movement to your spiritual practice is quite literally "incorporating" the practice – shifting the practice out of your mind and moving into and through your body as a whole. This one shift alone can transform your practice, not to mention transforming you as a spiritual being.

Many of us approach physical movement as though it were a means to an end. We do it because we "have" to, believing that if we didn't we'd gain weight or suffer from other physical ailments. The movement itself – the *process* of moving our bodies – is secondary to the results we hope to achieve by doing it.

Sometimes we approach movement as competition, either with others or with ourselves – trying to beat a record, or win a race, or excel at the activity. There are certainly benefits to doing movement regardless of your reason for doing it, but the spiritual benefits will come from engaging fully with the process itself, rather than with its collateral benefits.

The two key distinctions between spiritual movement and other forms of movement are your intention and your attention. You can change any movement into a spiritual practice simply by changing the reason you're doing it and where you place your attention while you're doing it. You can make any physical movement a form of meditation or prayer.

Just to get familiar with the feeling of connecting with your Soul *through* your body, you may want to start with a movement practice that was designed for that purpose. Yoga and Tai Chi are both great options for this. Some other choices might be walking meditation, breath work, Sufi dancing, or another form of ecstatic dance. Gabrielle Roth has a great program call The Wave which is a terrific way to experiment with soulful movement.

But you need not add any specialized forms of movement if you don't want to – you can simply modify your approach to the movement you already do by changing your intention and your attention while doing it. Shifting your intention is as easy as becoming aware of why you are doing a particular movement and then releasing any other agendas you may have besides the movement for the sake of movement itself. Whether you engage in a structured practice, like yoga, or a free form practice woven into your daily regime, any movement has the potential to become a blissful body prayer, if you approach it with that intent. Even strenuous movement that challenges you physically can become blissful when you devote your consciousness to that perspective, and you engage your heart and Soul in the effort.

Many traditions begin by dedicating the movement practice to something or to someone specific, and you may find it useful to center yourself and dedicate the practice before you start. In this way you can distinguish sacred movement from other movement you do during the course of a day. Activities such as stretching, walking, moving or lifting items, climbing, running, playing a sport, swimming or even bathing can become soulful movement if you are willing to take a moment to shift your intention and your attention.

Shifting your attention is just about bringing your focus back to the present moment while moving your body and really experiencing the movement. When you begin to stay fully present during your movement, really listening to your body and sensing your energy, you connect your heart and mind to your body, and allow your Spirit full participation in the physical reality of your body. This benefits both your body and your connection to Soul.

As always, consistency and willingness will play a major role in how deeply you can experience your soulful movement. Ask for guidance as you go. Your Sovereign Soul loves to engage with *all* of your being, especially your blissful beautiful body. After all, the experience of being physical is a profoundly spiritual one, and your Soul loves to engage with it!

Incorporating Purification

Purification is a foundational piece of any spiritual practice. In addition to regular purification of the body, you may want to add purification of the energy field, the heart and the mind. The body, both physical and energetic, as well as the heart and mind all function as filters – screening out environmental toxins wherever possible, and shaping what we are able to perceive and experience. Because of this, purification on all these levels is necessary in order to deeply receive and benefit from the guidance of your Sovereign Soul. If your filters are clogged, it makes it very difficult to sense and perceive changes in resonance.

I want to strongly urge you not to take on any form of body purification until you have researched it thoroughly, checked out the potential impact with your physician, and prepared yourself for it properly. Most purification activities when done for the first time can be uncomfortable (even dangerous), if approached without preparation and information. The key is to approach any process of purification with the proper respect, both for the process itself, and for your body. More is not always better.

That being said, there are as many ways to purify your body as there are ways to purify your home. You can use salt baths, salt water washes, sage, cedar, or sweet grass smoke, sound and music, visualization, breathing exercises, saunas and steam baths, skin brushing, tongue scraping, using a neti pot to cleanse your sinuses, clay, herbs and dietary cleanses to name a few. I won't recommend any particular modality for you because that will depend upon your physical condition and your lifestyle. Certain modalities will feel like a natural fit, while others may seem completely foreign to you. You can find more resources to support you in the Sovereign Soul Sanctuary online community at www.sovereignsoul.org. I would also suggest that you do some journaling and ask for guidance from your Sovereign Soul.

Once you have a sense of which modality you would like to work with initially, then it is time to begin your research, preparations and consultation with any medical professionals involved in your healthcare. This will give you both a spiritually guided plan, and one that is well-informed, balanced and healthy. Most of all, try to avoid any extremes. Purification activities should always be approached with respect, and in gradual stages. They are tremendously powerful, and even a small effort on your part will usually yield dramatic results, so be careful with them. Small but consistent application is the key.

Purification of your energy body, your mind or your heart can be approached with equal respect, but not necessarily with the same physical precautions that you've employed when purifying your physical body. Your energy field can collect toxins and negativity from the environment, as well as from any physical toxins you put into your body, so it needs to be cleansed usually daily. This can be as simple as a five minute clearing meditation that addresses each of the chakras in succession. Doreen Virtue has a wonderful book called "Chakra Clearing" that comes with a CD which has a morning and an evening clearing meditation, which I highly recommend. When I don't have time even for that, I will do a clearing that I call the "Smile" clearing. I just take a moment of silence, and then, one by one I picture each chakra as a face with a big beautiful smile on it, starting with the root chakra and working my way up to my crown chakra. So simple and so effective.

Another thing you can do to clear and protect your energy field is to work with your breath, and with natural elements. Just getting out into nature, or carrying stones and crystals with you can keep your energy fields relatively clear throughout the day.

Purification of your heart will mostly have to do with releasing and letting go of any hostilities, resentments, and energetic "ties" to people or situations that are draining you. A good deal of this work will be done when you cleanse your energy fields overall, but it can be helpful to release those thoughts and feelings as they come up and you recognize them. Some heart purification can be done with sound/tone and you will find that the more you can incorporate musical healing into your spiritual practice, the more clear and whole your heart center will become and remain.

Purification of the mind is one of the most neglected aspects of spiritual practice, but it will have a massive impact on your ability to live a Soul-centered life. Any thoughts, ideas and images that you are exposed to, or obsess about will clutter up your mind, and alter your ability to connect deeply with your Sovereign Soul. This is particularly true when it comes to things like watching the news before bed, following a sensationalized but negative news story, or indulging in gossip with acquaintances at the expense of another person or people. There are so many ways we clutter up our brains, and releasing that clutter consistently, every single day, will go a long way towards strengthening your spiritual foundation. Meditation, which we've discussed earlier, will support you in this clearing, but I think you will find that with mental clutter, as with all toxins, prevention is key. The more you can limit your exposure to negative, toxic thoughts and ideas, the easier it will be to purify your mind, and to keep that connection and communication with your Sovereign Soul open and flowing.

Spend some time exploring purification practices, and see if you can experiment with at least one for each area – body, energy body, heart and mind. There is a lot of information out there on purification practices to help you find what works for you, and, as always ask for help and guidance from your Sovereign Soul.

Incorporating Diet

What and how you eat will eventually become part of your spiritual practice, even if you don't start out that way. Diet and eating habits are such a visceral, tangible way that we love ourselves, and they reveal where we are strong and where we are vulnerable in that love. Whatever your relationship to love, as a force, that will also be your relationship to food, so there is much to learn about yourself and your Soul by examining and modifying your dietary practices.

Part of what you want to keep in mind when you get ready to approach this is that it will be an emotional exploration for you. It is for everybody. There are many wonderful books and programs and resources that examine the relationship between love and food. I can certainly not do this topic justice here. You can find more tools and resources to support you in the Sovereign Soul Sanctuary online community at www.sovereignsoul.org. All I want to do here is to remind you that your journey home to your Sovereign Soul is primarily a love story, and as such will require an exploration of your relationship to love and your willingness to shift that relationship to better align with the purposes of your Sovereign Soul.

Changes that you may need to make in order to align your dietary habits with the highest purposes of your Soul may include changing what you eat, where it comes from, how often you eat it, how present you are while you are eating it, when you eat and who you eat with. These are all ways that you can shift your eating habits in support of your connection to Soul, and eventually you will begin to look at each of these aspects in those terms.

When you are guided to, begin to journal around these questions, perhaps explore some of the fine books and resources on food and love, eating and the environment, or whatever you are guided to begin to look into. This will not be a sudden extreme move, but rather a gradual shift over time as you align more and more fully with the directives of your Soul. Allow for that to happen naturally, without self-judgment, or blaming. Your body and your Soul are naturally aligned in support of these sorts of changes, so you need only make yourself available to guidance and be willing to experiment with it. That's all that is required in order to see changes in your approach to food.

Working with the Breath

Breath work is a wonderful activity to add to your spiritual practice and will support all your other efforts as you go. If eating is about how we love, then breathing is about how we live. It represents our overall approach to life and we can receive tremendous spiritual benefits by working consciously with the breath to effect changes in how we live. Think of air as life force. If you take it in shallowly, if you ignore the fact that you take it in at all, if you hold your breath unconsciously, then these are all direct reflections on how you manage your own life force − how you relate to life as a whole.

A deep, slow, conscious, natural breath is the most healthful and most life affirming, but there are many, many different breathing practices designed to do a variety of things for you energetically. There are calming breaths, energizing breaths, purifying breaths and meditative breaths to name just a few. A good source of information on breathing exercises can be found in the yogic tradition – there is an entire yoga practice that centers on breath alone, so it is a good place to start your explorations. But even before you begin to explore adding consistent conscious breath work into your spiritual practice, you can simply bring your attention to your breath as often as you can during the day. Pay attention to how fluid or ragged your breath is, how you are holding your body while you breath, what part of the body you are breathing into, and how easy or difficult you find breathing. Just doing this as often as you think of it throughout the day will mark the beginning of some major shifts for you energetically. If you have a smart phone, you can even find applications that coach you through breathing exercises so you will have a coach available to you all the time.

As you observe your breath, you will begin to see how you relate to life. And as you alter your breath you begin to alter the way you live. Feel free to bring breath work to your work with movement, music and meditation. As a matter of fact, try to bring it to everything – how you breath when you sleep, how you breath when you eat, how you breath when you sit - this alone can be transformative. Remember that breathing is the one thing that you do continuously, day and night, asleep or awake, without even noticing you are doing it. Begin to notice. That's all you have to do to start. You can find more tools and resources to support you in the Sovereign Soul Sanctuary online community at www.sovereignsoul.org, and, as always, don't forget to ask for guidance and pay attention to your insights.

Setting up Structure to Support the Practice

Now that we've looked at the elements of a spiritual practice, it is time to begin to put some structure around the way that you practice. In order to be consistent with anything, you will need to have some way to track how often you do it, and to remind yourself when it is time to do it again. A spiritual practice, like any other practice, will initially rely upon your willingness to put that structure into place and to commit to acting upon it.

The first step in building a structure is to decide which elements to incorporate. It may be useful to review your journal and see what activities really supported you, or came most easily to you, and then begin with those. Don't try to implement too much all at once, but instead pick a few basic foundational elements and start there. You can add on as you develop the practice. It may be helpful in the beginning to write the practices on individual index cards so that you can mix and match.

Once you've decided upon a few basic elements, set a schedule for yourself – think about frequency, duration and also positioning – so you will be looking at how often you do each practice, how long you do it, and what day/time you do it. Purchase or make a calendar for the first three months of your practice and actually calendar each of the foundational elements.

Now it is time to install feedback mechanisms, so you can track what is working and what isn't – you will want to cross the activities off on your calendar each time you complete one, and reschedule any that you miss, so you can see later, when the best times were to actually complete the activity. You also want to schedule time immediately following each activity to journal on your experience. Each of these activities contains within it gems of information about you and about your Sovereign Soul. The only way to really integrate that information into your practice is to record it and to allow some time for exploration/insight. This is a really important aspect of developing a practice, because not everything you do will work out as you had intended it to, so you'll need an opportunity to process your discoveries. This will also keep your perspective centered in *exploratory* mode – out of judgment and blame – and instead completely captivated by discovery. So much of what you will be experiencing on this journey will be direct communication from your Sovereign Soul, but you'll likely miss out on a great deal of it if you have not scheduled time to record and explore it.

Implementing these basic structures will get you off to a good start in building a practice. Every three months (quarterly) you will want to review the practice and decide which elements are working, which need modification, which need reinforcement and which can be eliminated, at least for the time being. Every three months, review your practice, ask for guidance from your Sovereign Soul about next steps, and scan this chapter for inspiration and ideas. Be gentle with yourself as you begin to move into greater and greater alignment with your Sovereign Soul, and allow some time for false starts, set-backs and disappointment. These are all part of any journey, and the journey to your Sovereign Soul is no exception. Your Soul knows this, and is with you every step of the way.

If you get stuck, skip to the chapter called "What To Do When You Get Stuck!" and stay there for a while. Your Sovereign Soul has all the time in the world and she never leaves your side. She's been waiting for this all of your life, and she'll be right here, waiting for you when you are ready to approach a consistent committed practice again. So be as patient with yourself as she is, and know that you will eventually get there all in good time.

Chapter Six
Building Your Tribe

Now that you have created the space, the time and the means in your life to engage fully with your Sovereign Soul, it is time to explore the possibility of building a spiritual tribe to support your efforts. Before you struck out on your own as an independent spiritual seeker, you may have been involved in one or more of the organized religions. Looking back, you may find that it was not only the beliefs of that religion, but its structured nature that no longer appealed to you. The idea of handing over control to a structure or allowing others to dictate your beliefs to you may have been a big part of what you were leaving when you decided to leave. So you might find that the idea of "building a tribe" does not sound too appealing right now.

Ironically, it is your independence that makes a tribe so beneficial to you on your path - it's just one of those things you have to experience for yourself in order to perceive the value. You may be inclined to skip this chapter, either because of negative experiences with spiritual community in the past, or because you simply don't see a need for it. I hope, instead, that you will choose to give yourself the opportunity to explore the concepts in this chapter and work with some of the suggestions for a little while, just to see how they play out for you.

There are so many ways to approach community, and to benefit from interactions with others. You will find that the support of others can be of enormous assistance to you if you let it. It's also not just about how the tribe can benefit you, but also about what you have to offer them. Nobody lives in a vacuum and the insights, wisdom, humor and courage of others is always a welcome addition to any journey, even for the independent seeker. If you cut yourself off from that resource you dramatically limit your ability to receive the blessings that are available to you on the path, as well as your ability to bless others.

The chapters in this book have been very specifically ordered to give you a chance to strengthen your connection with your Sovereign Soul, and fortify your ability to discern true resonance with her. In the meantime, you've also been developing healthy boundaries, and a respect for the personal nature and privacy of your spiritual path. All of these factors must be in place before you can authentically expand your spiritual practice to include others.

This world holds a tremendous variety of spiritually motivated people with ideas and interactions that can impact you in a variety of ways. They offer these opportunities with varying levels of sincerity and positive intention. Because this is true, your ability to maintain a strong connection with your inner guidance, and a healthy respect for yourself and others will serve you well. Once you have learned how to maintain those healthy states while still interacting in an authentic way with others, you are then ready to explore a relationship with community as a spiritual force.

What the Tribe Can Offer You

A tribe is any larger group that represents larger interests than those of any one individual. Ideally it serves to both protect and inspire the individual by creating opportunities for exploration but with a much needed sense of stability in what appears to be an increasingly unstable world. The delicate relationship between the independent seeker and the tribe relies upon each respecting the other if the relationship is to survive.

The tribe can offer you a variety of opportunities to deepen your individual practice. It can function as a forum within which to explore concepts and to sound out your experiences in the loving, respectful presence of like-minded seekers. It can support your growth and the deepening of your spiritual experience by offering you resources, enthusiasm, understanding and wisdom as you approach things that are new to you. By interacting with the tribe, you can shorten your process of discovery. Members of the tribe can help you to broaden your approach to faith and prevent common missteps that may have held you back had you not had the benefit of their experience and their counsel. On an esoteric level, most traditions agree that the presence of other loving, supportive and wise souls provides a constant source of restorative energy – sometimes it can be enough just to know that they are there, keeping you moving, awake, aware and willing.

The spiritual community of a tribe can also offer you invaluable feedback from vantage points which may differ significantly from yours. Because of these differences, your tribe can sometimes spot aspects of your development that may have been invisible to you on your own. The truth is that the serious spiritual seeker may not only desire the company of an enlightened and evolving community – at a certain point on every path, they actually *need* this community if they are to go even one step further.

You will recognize that stage when you begin to feel a sense of urgency around establishing a tribe. You might even feel frustrated or profoundly lonely. When you reach that stage, you will feel a palpable sense of isolation which you may not have felt up until that moment. This is the gentle nudge of your Sovereign Soul guiding you to find a tribe that can function as a stabilizing force and a wellspring of resources and inspiration to support you in the next stage of your journey.

Trusting the Tribe

As much as you need the tribe, the tribe needs you. You have much to offer it, if you participate in an authentic and available way. Your ability to do this will be key to your spiritual development, and yet you may find yourself resisting the idea. You may hold back from participating fully or making any kind of commitment to the tribe, perhaps out of a basic mistrust. It could be because of past negative personal experiences with other spiritual communities or organizations, or it could be simply a mistrust of others in general. Either way, you will find that mistrust will be a barrier to your ability to bond with a spiritual tribe or benefit from your involvement with them. You might be so used to "going it alone" that any involvement with any kind of spiritual community (even one you build for yourself) could bring up some anxiety for you.

It can be scary to engage with other people about something as profoundly personal and important to you as your own Sovereign Soul. Truthfully, if you *were* actually out there on your own, without any guidance or assistance from your Soul, then your fear might be a necessary caution. But you aren't. You have the constant presence of your Sovereign Soul and her guidance is unerring.

She can bring to you the people that most support your highest good, and whom you can best serve with your own positive participation. She can alert you when something is not in alignment with your spiritual development – when you are getting distracted or off track. She can bring you to resources and insights and structure that will amplify your efforts exponentially. But you have to trust her. And you have to pay attention.

It is said that it is not enough to wander into the desert to receive the enlightenment. You must also commit to bringing the message back to your people. This truth is often overlooked by the independent seeker, especially one who doesn't even know who her "people" are. If you have been alone with your faith for a long time, if you have tried to reach out and connect with others before and failed, or if you have ever been vulnerable to a group that took advantage of your vulnerability for their own purposes, then you may have forgotten entirely what it is like to even have "people." You may have forgotten what it means to be part of a tribe, to have a spiritual family. But you have a responsibility to bring your truth back to the tribe. Your truth is needed by your people. Even if you haven't found a tribe of like-minded, like-hearted seekers yet, remember that your tribe is the tribe of humanity and they need your spiritual growth and insights now more than ever. Your mission, should you choose to accept it, is to grow as much as you can, love as much as you can and share as much as you can. That's it. That's all that is asked of you.

Fear and Spiritual Community

Humans are notoriously frail and flawed and vulnerable in their approaches to other humans. We experience so many of our higher intentions as challenging because of our unique histories and vulnerabilities. When you enter into community with others, those histories and vulnerabilities show up for you and for others in an amplified manner. This can be very scary and feel uncertain to you.

But you are *not* on your own out there. As much as you see yourself as an independent mystic and a solo seeker, you are not solo. You have never been solo. Regardless of which wisdom traditions you have embraced and explored, no matter how you define or describe God, or the Divine, the force and presence of your Sovereign Soul has always been with you, completely available to you. So you are not alone, even when you have perceived yourself to be so.

Guidance and the Tribe

Divinity supports you in every step you take along your path, including the step toward participating with others in any kind of spiritual community. As long as you remain available to the guidance within you, you will not lose your footing. You will not be deceived, betrayed, abused or neglected by the tribe you choose or create. If you allow your choices to be divinely guided, then any community, individual or group that seeks to harm or take advantage of you will become transparent to you. The work you have done and continue to do in strengthening your sense of self respect and respect for others will immediately alert you to any interactions that do not resonate with and strengthen that growing respect. Your work with privacy, and creating the ability, desire and willingness to maintain personal space internally and externally will prevent both your ideas and your physical being from being encroached upon.

You are learning to trust three things: yourself, your connection with your Soul, and your Sovereign Soul itself. As you do this, you will be drawn to tribes and individuals that are working on the same things.

It is important for you to know now, and to remember always, that the tribe is not an excuse to abdicate responsibility, or to relinquish personal empowerment and rely upon the responsibility of others. True spiritual community will offer only those ideas and activities that develop your sense of responsibility and strengthen your individual empowerment. In addition to that, the only thing that the community will request of you is that you support others in the community to do the same. When you operate from this basic framework you will have a very reliable way to understand the role of community and to identify the specific communities appropriate to your development.

Power and Community

It will probably be true that you find communities available to you which do not pass that litmus test, but which seem very compelling to you anyway. This is a natural byproduct of the spiritual domain and one that needs to be looked at before you proceed. There is, within each of us, a part that wants to abdicate the throne. We each have a small part of ourselves that is afraid of tremendous growth, tremendous joy, tremendous power and tremendous freedom. It is that small part that finds these sorts of groups compelling. It is as if they are whispering to that part of you "Hey, here is a chance for you to turn it all in and be free of it. Come this way, and we'll show you how you can go back to being a child again, before you knew enough to be in charge, before you had to make the decisions and live with the results. Let *us* take the wheel, and you can just relax and be safe,"

The larger the part of you that longs for a "return to innocence," the more compelling you will find the groups that offer that variety of spirituality. This probably accounts for the success of what we've called "cults" in the past, and why people have been willing to participate in their own self-destruction in the name of faith.

You should also be aware that there is a part like this in each of us, even if we don't acknowledge it, or even know it is there. Sometimes the only way we can see it clearly is to look at the quality of the decisions we've made over the course of our lives and to recognize in the nature of those decisions the state of mind that must have driven them.

If you made decisions in the past that offered too much control to other people, if you have sacrificed things that nourished your independence and fulfillment, then you can extrapolate from that that you may have a relatively large part of you that wants to abdicate the throne and return to your own innocence.

A huge step is just becoming aware of the presence and strength of that part of you. That's why I am bringing this up now, before you set out to find or create your tribe. This awareness will help you be better able to discern between a tribe that fosters responsibility and empowerment and one that tries to control or diminish you. If you consistently seek the higher guidance of your Sovereign Soul in this matter you will be presented with a multitude of different tribes that you can trust. You have freedom and choice to work with a variety of strengthening, deepening experiences and relationships on your journey, all of which will support your individuality and your empowerment.

Kinds of Tribes

The tribe can show up for us in a variety of ways, according to our needs at the time. It is not necessary to have only one cohesive community in order to be either fulfilled or committed to spiritual community as an element of spiritual practice. It is also not necessary for all the various communities in which you're involved to know or interact with one another. Some communities may meet some of your spiritual needs while others meet other needs. How much you can benefit from your involvement depends only upon the *quality* of your involvement. If you engage with the tribe in a committed way and you make yourself available to it fully within the context of what it can offer, then you will experience it as beneficial and fulfilling. The *way* you participate is the key to creating a *sense* of spiritual community in your practice. Who you show up as and how you show up makes all the difference.

First of all, you don't have to commit to all activities or ideologies within a tribe. For example, I might derive great spiritual satisfaction, spiritual growth, and form deep spiritual relationships by regularly attending a yoga class and committing to a home practice. That doesn't mean that I need to go live at an ashram and become a yogi. It also doesn't mean that my yoga practice is superficial and I am just getting some nice exercise there. Instead I have brought my full spiritual attention to that community and that commitment *as it relates to my individual path.* I have engaged fully with what was working for my higher development, and I've made a significant commitment not just to attend the class but to do the practice at home as well. In doing so, I've allowed the spiritual community that is the class to nourish my individual path. In addition, when I reached out to other members of the class and formed relationships that went beyond the boundaries of the class, I allowed the group to function as part of my tribe. So I would have created a spiritual community that existed for me, complete with practices, commitment and relationship without devoting myself to yoga as a comprehensive way of life. My participation could have been described as both guided and appropriate.

This is just one example of how you might draw upon only certain aspects of an existing community and still create that feeling for yourself of belonging to a tribe. Other examples could be found in coaching groups, creativity groups, book clubs, nature groups, or even aspects of other organized religions (spiritual retreats or choirs or volunteer work, for example). As a rule, any group that revolves around an activity that you really enjoy, and contains within it practices that foster consistency, creativity, connection to Soul and commitment are appropriate avenues for developing a sense of spiritual community.

Taking Stock

It may be useful for you to take stock of where you already experience community in your life, and see whether those communities not only support you socially, but also support you spiritually. It may surprise you to discover that you already have a spiritual tribe, but so far you haven't been consciously availing yourself of the support and inspiration they can offer. Take time to do some journaling on what community means to you, where you feel a sense of community, and how that community supports you or inspires you. Make a list of all the different kinds of communities in which you are involved (including your work if you work with others) and list the ways in which each one supports you. Look also at how you support it. Look at specific individuals within those communities and explore the potential that each might hold for a deeper, more Soul-driven connection. You may find out that you only need to deepen your commitment and expand your availability to communities and individuals with which you already participate in order to allow them to support you spiritually as well as socially.

Although you may begin by keeping your various communities separate from one another, you may eventually discover that this does not serve you. From an outside perspective it appears as though these would all be separate groups, fulfilling separate needs for separate reasons. But from your internal spiritual vantage point, they form one community – a single spiritual community in which you participate, at the center, as the hub of the wheel. This is true for each of us. It's as though each of us is a seed crystal and the rest of our true tribe crystallizes around us out of the saturated solution that forms our life. The essence of your life consists of relationships – literally how you relate to other people, things, and events. Metaphorically, if you align yourself with your Sovereign Soul's directives, you will discover that you become that seed crystal, and others who are aligned in a similar direction and who resonate with your current orientation to the Divine will show up and begin to form interlocked relationships, much the same way that salt forms around a string in a glass of saturated salt solution. So you form and inform your tribe by your own alignment and intention.

Your role, at this point is to look at who is "clustering" around you in alignment – who shows up in your life (so far) as relating to life and to the Divine in similar or complementary ways? Use your journal as an opportunity to explore this question and also to ask for guidance about ways that you might be able to deepen your commitment to those groups and individuals, and ways that you might make yourself more open, receptive and available to all that they can offer you. Ask to see what opportunities and hidden gifts lie within each relationship.

Combining Communities

At a certain point, when you have identified the groups and members of your unique tribe, and begun to experiment with expanding your commitment and availability to each of them, you will notice that overlap begins to happen. The work you do in one area will begin to impact the work you are doing in another. For example, your yoga practice will natively, inherently, inform your choir practice, even if you never articulate that for yourself or for others. It will change the way you breathe, the way you stand, even the way you manage energy and attention. These changes will then go on to change the way you sing in your choir. Every aspect of your spiritual practice will inform and develop all of the others. It is inevitable. And each relationship you have with a spiritual community will inform and develop the relationships that you have with the others.

At a certain point, the bringing together, or overlap, of the various communities that form your tribe will happen naturally and perhaps without your awareness. Your Sovereign Soul already sees that no matter how they came to you, essentially they all combine to form one single tribe for you. They may not be aware of it, and you may not be either, but your Sovereign Soul recognizes no division at the heart of it. As you become aware of this, a powerful way to honor your Soul's direction is to begin to consciously create opportunities for the various groups and individuals to interact with one another. In this way you tell yourself and your Soul that you are *ready to begin living at the center of your spiritual life,* to step into the role of "seed crystal" and allow the tribe to align around you. This willingness will profoundly impact the degree to which your tribe can support you and what you can offer them in return.

Bringing Down the Barriers

Your life experience can only be lived by you and only from within your point of reference. For you, this reference point is the only *true* reference point. Any compartmentalizing you attempt will be neither true nor effective. It may seem as though you offer different aspects of yourself to different communities – but the essential you is always present, always constant. You may have fears or concerns about bringing your "worlds" together but the more you are able to bring yourself authentically to the world from your own true reference point, the more authentic and rich your life experience will be.

The individuals within any community that are drawn to you enough to expand upon the relationship are drawn to the true, authentic, essential you. They are not drawn to whatever controlled or compromised version you believe that you have brought to the shared activity. People resonate with what is true and real in you, no matter how you met them, or who you think they are. So go ahead and let your various worlds collide. Seize the opportunity to explore what new connections can be created and alliances forged when you do.

Bring people from those various communities together as often as possible. Organize opportunities for this to happen, if you have to. Gather as many members of your spiritual community together at one time as you can. It can even be a completely "non-spiritual" activity if that feels most comfortable. It can be as simple as a potluck or a housewarming or a bonfire at the beach. It doesn't have to be lofty or elaborate. What matters is that you are allowing yourself to experience the members of your tribe all in one place at one time and letting yourself experience what it is like to feel that support all around you. This may be the first time you've ever felt that caliber of community before, and it's worth a little effort and energy to create the experience. Allow yourself to feel the love of being surrounded by people who share your journey and to offer them the opportunity to meet and interact with one another. It has the potential to be a powerful experience that can benefit all involved on multiple levels.

Alliances and Points of Connection

Even if you do not gather members from your various communities all together at one time in one place, it is still useful to find as many ways as possible to create alliances and single points of connection. Even if just a few members from each community have something in common, it is worthwhile to connect those few members and enjoy a shared experience. There is great power and opportunity in allowing these individuals to ally with one another, and being the vehicle for that opportunity engages you with them on a different level.

It is also useful to strengthen individual points of connection with members of a spiritual community outside of the context of that community. It can be as simple as inviting someone from your art class to coffee, or volunteering to help them with a yard sale. It doesn't have to be a big ceremonial thing. All you are trying to do is to strengthen and broaden the context within which this person relates to you. You are simply changing the tone of the relationship so that it better aligns with your more conscious focus. This can deepen your relationship with each of them, and also allow you to function as a bridge between people who may not have had the opportunity to meet any other way.

Surprisingly, as you see the various elements of your spiritual identity interacting in a supportive and empowering manner out in the world, it becomes easier and easier to allow those aspects of your personality to support and empower one another internally. There is tremendous value when you complete the circuit between the inner world and the outer manifestation of that world. If you have underestimated either your ability to make this happen or the potential benefit from having done so, then you are in for a wonderful surprise.

Creating New Communities

As you develop spiritually, and particularly as you experience the tremendous satisfaction not only of participating in spiritual communities, but bringing together members from various communities, you may feel inspired to create a new spiritual community around an activity or emphasis that you haven't been able to find already in existence. This is not an uncommon thing, and usually results from wanting to deepen or expand some aspect of a community to which you already belong.

As you find yourself craving this expansion, you may realize that there are other people from other spiritual communities in which you participate who would also benefit from and enjoy the community you are contemplating creating. Do not be afraid to invite people to participate with you in your new group, even if you know them from different environments. Stay open to Divine inspiration, and be willing to simply put it out there.

If you find that there is no interest from anyone in your various communities, don't be afraid to cast a wide net and invite the general public – post a flyer, put a free ad online or put a small classified ad out in a publication that is a resource for like-minded people. Make the process of inviting people as simple as possible, and, if you feel more comfortable, simply invite them to attend a single event so you can get a sense of the dynamic of the group, as they will be strangers to you.

Make sure that you collect contact information at or before the event, and then, if you find you resonate more with certain people than with others, you can contact them privately to invite them to additional events, or to suggest participating in the activities in a regular fashion. Be sure, as you conceive of the nature of your new community, that you remember to try to include opportunities for the four C's – Consistency, Creativity,

Connection and Commitment. Any group based upon spiritually-aligned intentions that presents opportunities for each of these elements will be an enriching one for participants.

Resources for Inspiration

If there is not a natural and evident extension of any of the spiritual communities in which you already participate that would make a good basis upon which to found a new group, you can look to several resources to inspire ideas. One resource would be your own journal. Hopefully, as an independent spiritual seeker you have been using a journal regularly to chart your course, acknowledge your successes and explore your options. Within your journal you will probably find numerous areas in which you have expressed a desire to go deeper, but have not yet explored. These ideas are Divinely inspired, and while you may have back-burnered them at the time, perhaps now it would be appropriate to pull them out, dust them off and finally give them the attention they deserve.

Chances are, if you have wanted to dig more deeply into a particular spiritual subject, there are probably other seekers out there who would be equally interested. And if you can't find an existing group with whom to explore, chances are they haven't been able to either. When you initiate something like this, you become a resource to others as well as to yourself. By creating the space to do this particular exploration, you not only bring together others who are on the path, but you allow all mutual resources and approaches to be shared and developed.

Most importantly, know that you don't have to be an expert in the subject to be successful in your efforts – you just have to be clear on your own intention in creating the group, and willing to share your personal experiences and resources with others who are willing to do the same. It can be as simple as a meet-up for coffee at a local coffee-house once a month, or as elaborate as weekly pot-luck at people's homes on a rotating schedule. Trust that it will find its own level; all you have to do is initiate it.

Once initiated, you will find that these things grow and develop over time. The most casual sporadic meeting between seekers can grow into a group dynamic that supports the members and expands their possibilities in a way you never could have anticipated and that none of the participants could have achieved on their own. I cannot overstate the value of creating, aligning with and participating in a group that truly cares for, respects and empowers its members. This alone will revolutionize your spiritual practice – reaffirming and strengthening your ability to trust other people, to show up authentically, to respect and be respected by others, and to expand fearlessly in a safe environment. If you would like to explore how best to create or expand your tribe you can find more tools, resources, and kindred spirits to support you in the Sovereign Soul Sanctuary online community at www.sovereignsoul.org.

You are still a solo seeker, as the path that you will take will always be unique to you. You will continue to draw only upon sources and traditions that resonate specifically with you, but you will have fostered a sense of belonging and a willingness to share your unique path with others, thereby enriching the experiences of all concerned. This represents a profound shift for the solo seeker, and should be acknowledged and celebrated!

Chapter Seven
Stepping Into Service

Every organized religion offers the seeker an opportunity to participate in some form of service, and with good reason. Every spiritual seeker will find that the first step toward spiritual development is to connect with the Divine, and the next step, in order to complete the circuit, is to put that connection into action and to serve others. Because this is such a crucial element in spiritual development, every major wisdom tradition will include some component of their practice that involves stepping into service to others. Yet, the independent spiritual seeker almost always overlooks this element, and usually to the detriment of both the seeker and the practice itself.

Faith in Action

Spiritual insight is a wonderful thing, but until you can put it into action, and bring your expanded self to the world, you have limited the impact your insight can offer you. Stepping into service is how you put your faith into action for the well-being of another. The act of participating in service to others is what allows the seeker's faith to deepen and develop. It serves to free a spiritual practice from the limited confines of the seeker's mind, heart and body, and lets it ripple out into the world for the benefit and inspiration of others.

You may already have experienced this as you explored participation in spiritual community. Service to the community would have been a natural expression of faith, but in that form, service was probably approached as a by-product of the experience, rather than the experience itself. When you step fully, consciously into service as an aspect of your own spiritual practice, then you cultivate an even deeper aspect of service – one that could be described as devotional. Your contribution to the well-being of another or others IS your prayer, it is your devotion, your meditation. When you experience devotional service as part of your spiritual practice, you offer your attention, your energy and the force of your being to another that they might benefit from your offering. This is a sacred act that transcends basic duty or morality. Acts of this nature become acts of union with the Divine – when you step into service, you literally step into the shoes of your Sovereign Soul – you are acting on earth as the ambassador, the emissary of your Soul. This is powerful work and if you truly embrace it, you will find it to be exponentially satisfying and fruitful.

Service as Distinct from Servitude

For many people in the modern world, the word "service" has been distorted. When I speak of "service," you may imagine some great and noble act with potential for massive impact – like the work of Mother Teresa, for example. You might be intimidated by the idea of service, even asking yourself if you are worthy to serve. "What can I possibly have to offer?" you may be asking yourself right now, if your impression of what it means to serve has been inflated by popular culture.

The opposite, (and equally popular) distortion of the concept of "service" is to associate it with servitude – so we hear the word, but we link it to the idea of being dominated, controlled or humiliated by others. Careers typically categorized as being in the "Service Industry" are basically careers where you wait on other people. Within this context, the concept of service is not a collaborative dynamic, and you are not perceived as an authority in your area of expertise. You may be the best waiter or the best doorman or the best chauffer or the best butler or the best maid or the best concierge in the world, but essentially working in the "Service Industry" places you under the authority of others for their purposes. Of course, being under the authority of others is true in most jobs that feature a power hierarchy rather than a collaborative structure, but you usually answer to specific people higher up in the company. Front line positions in the "Service Industry" must answer to any random stranger who walks through the door and pays for the service. Certainly it is not my intention to diminish the value of those positions, or the worth of individuals who make their living employed in these industries, I do want to be clear that in these industries the word "service" has taken on a very different meaning than it would have in the context of your spiritual practice. So what does it mean to step into service spiritually?

Taking on the Mantle

As with soulful movement, soulful service is primarily distinguished by your intention to represent Spirit by your act, and by the consistent, focused attention you give to the act. As with movement, you will find that although it is useful to serve wherever you can, whenever you can, when you do it consciously

– when you deliberately *take on the mantle of your Soul* and step in, on behalf of the Divinity within you, to serve the well-being of another, you have done something distinctly different than simply performing the act itself. By taking on the mantle, you have completed the circuit, delivered the message, made the import of your Sovereign Soul manifest in the world and available to the greater good of all. This is as profound as it is powerful, and having done so will have a lasting impact on your being, and your spiritual development.

At first you will find it valuable to serve in very focused, specific ways. Although ultimately your spiritual development will allow you to become a blessing to the world in everything you do, it may be helpful in the beginning to focus your service on specific things that you care deeply about and to which you are willing to commit your time, energy, and attention. Take some time now to journal around what you truly care about. What in the world would you like to see transformed and how can you be a part of it consistently? What do you care about most? Is it the planet? The people? The animals? How specific can you be? You'll find additional tools and resources to support you in exploring this topic in the Sovereign Soul Sanctuary online community at www.sovereignsoul.org.

By laser-focusing your efforts and consciously offering your time and energy and attention to those causes that most deeply affect you, you activate the true power of service in this world. In doing so, you become a conduit, a portal through which the energy of your highest intention can become manifest – actual physical changes will happen in the world because of your intention, your conscious attention, and your willingness to take the steps and complete the actions that are needed for them to take place. When you take on the mantle and step into service, you become the ambassador of your highest vision. In doing so, you step forward to represent not only that possibility, but your own commitment to it and your willingness to bring it about.

For example, if you serve food at a homeless shelter, you are the literal representation of the possibility of an end to world hunger. If you march on Washington for animal rights, then you are the ambassador from a world where animals are treated with dignity and respect. You *stand for* that world. So you are more than sum of your acts – your acts themselves speak to a greater, more comprehensive possibility. Your acts of service have ritual significance. It is important for you to really get that – that the message is as important as the act itself. The world needs the message as much as (if not more than) it needs the material effect of the act.

To be of service, then, is a tremendously powerful thing to be, and a little goes a long way. Small acts of service have potentially great impact. You need not actually solve world hunger in order to represent the possibility of a world without hunger and to have the truth of that possibility ripple out from your act of service into the hearts and minds of others.

To be of service you also do not need to abdicate your authority or disempower or diminish yourself in any way. In truth, you actually further empower yourself when you witness how much you really have to offer the world, and how much the world needs your testimony. Because that's what it is. When you serve the well-being of another, you are testifying on behalf of a better world. You bear witness not to the problem, but to the solution. And that is a seat of power. When you allow your Sovereign Soul to work through you to transform the world, you expand as a being. And you can do it simply by signing a petition or knitting some gloves or even sending money. As long as your intention is to serve and your attention remains consciously focused upon and devoted to that goal, you are stepping into service. Your act becomes faith made manifest - you have delivered your Soul's message and completed the circuit.

Ways to Serve

You may already be serving others somehow – but perhaps only doing so out of obligation, or a sense that it is the "right" thing to do. You can easily shift this service into Soulful service by taking a moment before you begin to shift both your intention and your attention. As with soulful movement, you may find it helpful to actually dedicate your act of service to an individual or a group of individuals.

If you are not already in service to anyone or anything, then you may find it valuable to explore what causes or individuals you feel particularly drawn to, and then look into a way to participate on their behalf. Once you have identified those whom you feel called to serve, and discovered a means by which to do so, the next step is to calendar the time (structure, remember?) and consciously set your intention (perhaps with a dedication) before each act of service. While you are in service, you can participate in whatever way you feel called, all the while remembering that your participation is your prayer for the well-being of whomever you are serving on behalf of your beautiful and mighty Sovereign Soul. I cannot adequately describe the sensation of experiencing yourself as an emissary on behalf of your own Soul – experiencing your act of service as an offering in gratitude for all those that have served you during the course of your life, both human and non-human – and allowing yourself to step into the expanded role of the "World Server" – this is a huge and intensely pleasurable endeavor.

Challenges of Service

Be forewarned that service is also often challenging. You may confront all the smaller parts of yourself as you seek to expand into the larger, more inclusive aspects of who you know yourself to be. You may find obstacles and barriers specifically designed to get you to turn back, to abandon your attempt to serve another. You may find yourself asking "Who am I to be stepping into the shoes of the Divine?" Alternately, you may find your ego trying to co-opt your efforts, and feel yourself puffing up with self-aggrandized attitudes – your ego may cause you to feel superior to those you serve, or to feel smug for being such a "good person" by serving as much as you do. The ego is crafty and will stop at nothing to try and keep you small – to prevent your union with the most expansive aspects of your being. Just be aware, going in, that it may not be smooth sailing all the way. As with all aspects of your practice, your journal will be a huge resource to you. It will keep you honest, and humble and alert. Be sure to calendar time to journal after each act of service so that you can record your experience and check in with yourself and your Soul to see how you are doing.

Transforming Your Work into Service

If you find that you are currently not involved in any act of service, but do not find yourself able to add any service opportunities to your already full schedule, there is another way that you can bring the element of service into your daily life and into your practice.

Take a look at where you commit money to charities – is it something that you do consciously, or something that is haphazard – whoever gets to you first and in the most compelling way gets your cash. Write out all the charities you regularly contribute to, as well as the ones that you have sporadically supported and see if there is an existing theme. Is there one cause, or group of individuals or creatures that you are particularly drawn to support? If so, then look at how you contribute. Is it annually? Is it monthly? Or is it random? See if there is a way that you can commit even a small amount monthly in an automatic withdrawal format to the causes that you care most about. Then collect images of those whom you support with your donations and bring them to wherever you work.

Now your regular work has become something that you are doing in service to someone else – you can practice dedicating each day to an individual, or to the group or the cause by visualizing your work that day as being directly in service to them. This really only works if you are on auto-withdrawal though – you have to create the sensation that a certain percentage of each days effort is specifically done in service to someone or something, on behalf of the highest most expanded aspect of yourself. If you don't have it set up as percentages, it is still worth doing, but not quite as effective. For example, one of the causes that I am most passionate about is animal welfare. So I dedicate a percentage of my income to specific animal welfare causes that do what I cannot personally do. Then I dedicate my work as service on behalf of the animals that I support. In this way, all work becomes service, just as all life becomes prayer.

The Selfless Gift

Take some time to explore where you are already in service. See if there is a way that you can shift your existing service into conscious sacred service or to add elements of service to your life, if you are not already in service to another. You can also count the service that you offer your loved ones, but not exclusively – because you are in an energetic dynamic with your loved ones, and you each serve one another, the energy is valuable but does not replace the need for pure service.

When we speak of sacred service, this is energy, time, attention and resources that you offer another with whom you have no expectation of return. It is an offering, and the one that you serve does not owe you anything, and will not be serving you in kind. Others in your life will certainly serve you, and many of them will do so without expectation of return, but the one or ones that you offer sacred service to will not be the ones returning the favor. This will be a selfless gift on your part – it will not be done for status, out of duty, or with expectation of any kind. Instead, you will show up as Spirit shows up, purely giving, purely loving, and completely fulfilled in the act itself. This is how you step into the shoes of your Sovereign Soul. This is how your Soul has always shown up for you, how she has always served you. Now it is your turn, and you are passing it on, with reverence, with gratitude and with devotion. This is how you thank God – through your service to those in need. This is how you embody love.

Take some time to explore your options here, and listen to what you feel called to do. When you show up to serve – whether in a way that you've served before, a brand new opportunity, or simply changing your intention and awareness around your work so that you can devote a portion of your income to service – do so with an open heart and a great sense of the bounty you represent. You are the portal through which the great abundant blessings of Spirit can flow out into the world. You are developing yourself consciously, spiritually, through your good works, and you are celebrating your ability to do so. The more you expand as a spiritual being, the greater your opportunity to serve. This is what it is all about, so enjoy it and embrace it – because it is purely inspired by the very best and most beautiful part of who you are.

Chapter Eight
What To Do
When You Get Stuck

It is true, without exception, that you will eventually get stuck. Every seeker does. Getting stuck is just part of the process. The trick is not to avoid getting stuck (which is impossible) but to learn how to approach stuckness – what to do with your mind and your heart and your body when you do get stuck. Accepting the stuckness and practicing the most useful approach to it will be helpful both in lessening the frequency with which become stuck and the duration and intensity of the general stuckness.

Imagine that instead of reading a book about a journey, you were physically on a journey that was taking you a very long distance through some very strange terrain. Imagine that at different points along the way the terrain became more and more harsh and daunting from your vantage point. The path became steep, the landscape seemed to do its best to discourage you from your travels and the weather shifted in such a way as to create even more of a challenge just in the moving from one point to another.

Hostile Territory

For many seekers, this place in the journey, this exact spot, is where the terrain feels most unforgiving, and most hostile. The sheer cliffs of overwhelm may be looming around you, and the stinging rain of external influences (time and energy drains) may be pelting you ceaselessly.

Maybe you've put this book down for a few days (or a few weeks), as you recoiled, daunted by the apparent enormity of the task at hand. Maybe you started strong but just got distracted or detoured for a while. Maybe a long while. Every spiritual seeker, whether firmly clutched to the bosom of an organized religion, or making the trek, out there on their own, comes to a place in the path where the way becomes hard, and the seeker sits down. She can simply go no further. But neither can she turn back. She's stuck there. So she simply sits down.

The Plateau

Maybe you are there now. If not, know that at some point you will be. This is part of the process. It does not fit nicely into the Western trajectories of success and goal-setting and achievement. It does not respond to platitudes or pep talks. This is part of the "who" that you are, right now, as you stand on the path of your spiritual evolution. This is the shadow side of a spiritual life, and it shows up whenever we begin to make real changes on any level.

Dieters, people working with an exercise regime, athletes, writers, artists, parents, couples in love - basically anyone who is moving from one chapter of their lives into the next - will find their way to this place. The plateau. The place between what you want and what you are letting go of to get it. This place is the land of limbo, the sluggish place of non-movement. This is the territory where you might find yourself trying actively to thwart your journey, in a futile attempt to return to what you know. And, you may be surprised to discover that all of this heel dragging, and negotiating and procrastinating and detouring – all of it – all of this is perfectly fine.

You are exactly where you need to be. So you don't need to try to move yourself out of this place. You don't need to effort and struggle and freak out. You don't need to give yourself a stern talking to, or get your ducks in a row or beat yourself up, or draw any conclusions whatsoever. No matter how it may look to you as though you are "back sliding," know that this place is not the same place you've just left. And this place is also not the place to which you journey. This place is simply a station on the way.

Stopping at the Station

Imagine that you are literally traveling across country and on the next leg of the journey you were to travel by train. So you've made your way to the train station, and the weather may be poor, you may be alone, sitting on your suitcase, out on the platform, the wind whipping down the tracks, nobody in sight, no posted train schedule, and no evidence of any train at all, maybe ever.

No matter how certain you are of your desire to reach your destination, no matter how clearly you received the directions to this train station, no matter how many times you've checked your watch, you are still going to go through a phase where you doubt every aspect of your being there.

And the longer you sit on your suitcase, out in the biting wind, alone, with nobody to ask, the more you begin to question the whole thing. Am I in the right place? Is there really a train scheduled? Maybe it already came and I missed it? Why is there nobody else here? Why is there no schedule posted? Maybe I've been misled. Why is there no one in charge of this? Was there ever a train here? Maybe this is an abandoned station. Maybe I've lost my way.

You can see how this happens. In truth, the train is on its way, and when it gets here, when you climb aboard into the warm, well-lit car, when they serve you a nice hot cup of cocoa and they punch your ticket, when you feel the comfort of the train car rocking gently, side to side, as that train begins to climb the mountain pass, when you see how quickly the trees flash by the window, and you notice how beautiful the snow is as it falls, when you climb higher and higher into the mountains, and all around you the other passengers talk quietly among themselves, or sleep, or read, when you settle into the effortlessness of the journey at this stage, you will wonder why you ever doubted the train at all. And you will smile as you look back and remember how you almost considered trying to make your way back to whatever you had left, so frightened were you, sitting there, alone on that platform in that seemingly abandoned train-station, waiting.

The Waiting is the Hardest Part

So this is where you are when you reach the plateau. Here there is nothing left to do but wait. Intellectually you know it, but emotionally you feel you must do something. Waiting and *not knowing* is so profoundly uncomfortable that doing *anything*, even worrying, or backtracking, sounds better than just sitting there, waiting. The truth is that the train is right on schedule and you have come exactly to the very spot where you need to be. You are on time, it is on time, and it offers you exactly what you need, but it has its own schedule, and you can neither confirm nor control that schedule.

In the center of that feeling of not knowing, and being completely helpless, you will be tempted to try to regain control in one of two ways. First you may be tempted to abandon your vigil, because even if you are wrong to do so, at least you had the small amount of control that making a decision, any decision, affords you.

The second thing you may be tempted to do is to blame and shame yourself. This is particularly tempting, because it gives the illusion that you have or had some control all along, and if you had just done things differently, then you wouldn't be in this God Forsaken Place!!! So this has the dual purpose of both paralyzing you from taking any action, *and* giving you the feeling of having not completely lost control. As though you might prevent this feeling of discomfort by learning your lesson this time and then doing it differently next time. So that feels like something.

Do your level best while you are here at the station to identify both of these temptations for what they are and simply let them pass by. Were you to entertain either of these strategies, you would not influence the train's innate schedule, you would not regain actual control over the timing of the situation, and you would not relieve yourself of your discomfort. This is because you are already where you need to be, and simply waiting on a train that is on its way to you, even as you sit there, shivering on that cold, abandoned platform.

The Third Option

Ignore the first two temptations, and look for the third option. You have a third option, and that option is faith. Just knowing that this is a normal part of the journey, and that there is nothing you need to do except to keep believing in the train, waiting for the train, looking down the tracks in the full knowledge that the train is on its way, that is enough. This book, this chapter in this book, is, in our metaphor, an envelope that you find taped to the locked door of the station. You open the envelope, and inside you find a letter. The letter reads as follows:

"Dear Beloved Seeker,

Do not worry. You have come to the right place. You are right on time, and the train is on its way, even though you cannot see it yet. It is a wonderful train and it's worth the wait, but unfortunately you'll be waiting alone and you may be waiting here for a while. Please, try to make yourself as comfortable as possible while you are here – try to find a spot with a little shelter from the wind, and don't lose hope, no matter how long it takes for your train to get here. If it helps, spend some of your time imagining the train, imagine what it will be like once you've climbed aboard, put your suitcase under your seat, and you are resting, warm and comfortable while the train carries you quickly and safely to your destination.

Spend your time and your energy keeping yourself comfortable and keeping your thoughts on that train, Seeker. That is all you that you are required to do right now. It's that simple. There is nothing else you need to do. The Sovereign Soul Express is on her way to you, right now, moving swiftly, clickety-clacking steadily, rocking her way across the landscape, every second getting closer and closer to you. Your only job right now is to wait and to wait in the most comfortable, joyful way that you can manage.

The wind will keep blowing, the rain will sting your cheeks, it will get dark and you will be sitting here alone for what feels like a long, long time. All of that is part of the journey, nothing is wrong with it, nothing is wrong with you, nothing is wrong with the train. You have one job to do and that is to wait, and to wait in the best way you know how. To wait in faith. And to remind yourself and remind yourself and remind yourself what it is that you are waiting for. Because what you are waiting for will make all of this worthwhile. You will not regret having waited. I promise. I give you

My Deep and Abiding Love,

Your Sovereign Soul"

So, this is the plateau. This is where you find yourself ignoring what you thought you had already learned, forgetting what you thought you knew, trying out old bad habits, almost testing yourself to see if maybe there might possibly be a way back to the old you. The plateau likes to show up mostly in the portion of the journey that looks at how you handle time. The reason is that so much of the way we "manage" time is locked deep within our unconscious minds, and so much of the way we live speaks to the parts of us that are, as of yet, unlived. So shining the light of awareness into those areas can create a certain amount of sluggishness, and maybe some fear, doubt and resistance. More than anything those needs would prefer not to be rousted from their secret hiding places.

You must remember that there is a part of you that really believes that the ways you've figured out to meet (or even partially meet) your needs are working and it is that part of you that does not want to give those ways up. When you begin to work with getting conscious about how you spend your time, that is the part of you that will send out the big guns, if only to scare you off. And when they do, you will feel yourself on that abandoned train platform, literally "stuck in your tracks" and unable to get anywhere, with no idea what to do, if anything.

This is all perfectly normal. This is where we give "feet" to our faith, as they say. This is where the rubber meets the road. This is where, for lack of a better word, you are tested. Your faith is tested. You, yourself, are the one doing the testing, so it may be helpful for you to know that, but the testing feels absolutely real, and it is important that you recognize that as well. Who better to test you than yourself? After all, you know all the places where you are most vulnerable. Do not be lulled into a false sense of security simply because your challenges are of your own design. There are three priorities for you right now.

Three Priorities

First, make yourself as comfortable as possible with *not knowing*, so that you can bear the wait. Activities that achieve this may include anything in the self-care arena – bathing, sleeping, walking, getting out into nature even briefly, making sure you are hydrated, and well rested, and fed good healthy food while you wait. The watch word here is "Nourish!!"

Second, spend as much of your emotional and intellectual energy as you can envisioning what it is that you are waiting for. That may mean reading inspirational texts, journaling about your spiritual journey, listening to uplifting music, watching uplifting programs, going to a church, temple or any place of worship, whatever it takes, whatever can feed your spirit while you wait. The goal right now is to return your mind to your mission over and over again, until your thought process naturally finds its way there, regardless of the circumstances.

Priority three is to keep an eye out for the train itself. This means continuing to look down the track, listening for the whistle, maybe placing your hand on the tracks themselves to detect even the faintest of vibrations announcing the train's imminent arrival.

While you wait, keep looking for signs of the presence of the Divine and things that would signal the right time to move on to the next stage, the next chapter of the journey. If you can manage it, keep a joyful vigil, paying the utmost attention to anything, no matter how small, that would indicate the wait will soon be over, and that you will be directed on to the next part of your journey.

Pay attention to your dreams, to your physical energy, to your prayers and meditations. Pay attention to conversations overheard, and opportunities that might arise unexpectedly, signaling some movement on your part. You are not manufacturing these events in response to your eagerness to proceed. Instead, you are holding yourself open to them, allowing for them, watching and waiting for them with enthusiastic anticipation.

These are the three things to be mindful of while you wait — keep yourself as comfortable as possible, turn your thoughts to that which you await, and keep a joyful vigil for signs of its imminent arrival. Do not expect these activities to shorten the wait, or to control the outcome in any way. Only anticipate that they will make the waiting time as enriching and meaningful as waiting can be. And that, while you wait, you will be renewing your commitment and strengthening your faith with every day that passes. That, too, is part of what you have been waiting for.

Obviously, you'll move in and out of these three priorities to different degrees at different times, depending upon your ability to accept the situation and relinquish control. This waiting, the plateau, is an important and necessary part of the journey, and your learning to meet your needs on all three fronts while you wait is an important part of your being able to navigate through the rest of the plateaus that you encounter in this life journey. Throughout your expansion, you will often have to wait. This is just one more opportunity for you to learn how to do it well.

Return to this chapter and reread it whenever you get to a plateau in your journey. Let it serve to remind you of the purpose of the plateau and of your highest, best response to it. In time you will learn to recognize not only the big, but the little plateaus as you become more and more proficient in responding to the plateaus with your faith.

A Few Last Thoughts

You've probably gathered by now that working through this book you've actually not come to the ending of anything. Your journey of spirit, this love story that is your ever-deepening reunion with your Sovereign Soul, will never end. It will never be over, and you will never have completed that work.

As much as this book has been able to point out some of the gathering places, the common ground of such a journey, you already know that each journey is unique. The general aspects, exercises, challenges and approaches are nothing but a rough sketch – some broad strokes to assist you in creating your own perfect map to your Sovereign Soul. It is a map that only you can discover and one that only you can understand and follow.

So there is no destination, at least not one that is separate or distant from you. The journey itself has been your destination all along, and the one you seek, your own Sovereign Soul, has been your constant companion. You have learned what most connects you to her, and then you have practiced creating those circumstances and opportunities for yourself wherever you were able. If you were to return to the beginning of the book and start "all over again" you would still not cover the same territory twice. This is because you are not now who you were then, the last time you approached that leg of the journey. There are beautiful secrets that only your beloved Sovereign Soul can reveal to you. Some she has already revealed, but there are so many more to come, so many more to look forward to.

There is no way to remove yourself from this journey – all you can do is participate in it more or less willingly, more or less consciously, with more or less joy. Once you accept that the journey itself is inevitable, then you can fully apply yourself to the task of deciding *how* you want to make the journey. Your Soul will not be denied, she will not go away, she will not abandon or forsake you. She is ever with you, ever available to you, and ever active on your behalf. This I know with certainty. So all you have to do is to decide and to keep deciding what sort of a traveling companion you want to be. Will you be the companion that works in partnership and with pleasure as you make your way? Will you arrange your participation so that the lines of communication are open and you are available to them whenever possible? Will you deliberately meet each day with the knowledge of how vital this journey is, and be open to the possibilities that each day holds for you? Are you the companion that says "yes!" or the companion that says "no!"? These are all choices that are yours, and only yours, and they renew themselves each and every day. No matter what you chose yesterday, you can choose differently today.

Little by little you will come to feel and understand that your faith was never meant to be an accessory to your life. It's not there to enhance the experience of life – to make your relationships better, or to make the world seem safer, or to give you something to hope for. Although it can and does offer you those things, they were never the purpose of faith. They were never the function of faith. Your life is not the reason for your faith. Instead, your faith is the reason for your life.

Your relationship to the Divine and your expansion into alignment with your Sovereign Soul are the purpose for everything else in your life. Every relationship, every challenge, every hope that you hold is there only as an expression of the Divine. Each represents an opportunity for you to come to know your Sovereign Soul more intimately and to express that knowledge, that love, more freely and more generously.

If you have truly committed yourself to placing your Sovereign Soul at the very center of your life, and arranging your life around that one relationship – your relationship with the Divine - then you will begin to experience the wonder and beauty that a Soul-centered life can offer you. It is something that can't be dictated to you, it can't be enforced or insisted upon by another, and nobody else can make it happen for you. This is between you and your Soul and God. But I promise you, once you get a taste of it, you will never want to give it up. It's a way of looking at everything – through the lens of how it affects your relationship with Spirit – that brings so much grace, and compassion and joy with it that you won't have any doubt that it is worth whatever you have to do to sustain and expand upon it.

The map is a treasure map, and the treasure is your journey itself, your unique path deep into the heart of your faith, and your spiritual expansion and expression as you find your way there. It is my prayer for you that you will be fortified by your journey, and that you will return to this map, this love story, over and over again, as you make it uniquely yours.

If you are craving a next step, please visit the Sovereign Soul Sanctuary online community at www.sovereignsoul.org for access to additional resources, worksheets, assessments, audio programs, supplemental materials to the book, access to a private facebook group and different levels of coaching and support from which to choose.

The most important thing I can tell you, in closing, is that you don't need to do anything "right" and that there is no wrong way to come home to your Soul. Wherever you are, however you are, your Sovereign Soul can and does use all of it. Nothing is wasted. Nothing is lost. No exceptions. You are fine, you are right on time, and all is well. You can trust yourself and you can trust your Sovereign Soul. My dear, dear seeker, your journey is not a test. You are not being judged...you are being welcomed.

Welcome home.

About the Author

Kaite McGrew is a transformative spiritual coach, intuitive and founder of the Sovereign Soul Sanctuary online community. As an independent mystic, Kaite has made it her personal mission to support spiritually independent women in finding and fostering their own faith that fits. Her philosophical explorations span from the major wisdom traditions to psycho-spiritual models, New Thought principles, and nature-based philosophies including modern deism. For Kaite, there is no "one size fits all" version of faith – faith is a custom job.

Kaite currently lives in Northern California and shares her home at the edge of a eucalyptus grove by the sea with an amazing, enlightened dog and an eerie blue-eyed cat.

About the Illustrator

Geoffrey Mundon is a multi-media artist whose work, in addition to drawing and painting, includes wire sculpture, wood carving and traditional Hawaiian arts such as bone jewelry and printmaking. Currently he lives on the side of a mountain in Hawaii with his beautiful wife and two brilliant and charming daughters under the ever-watchful gaze of their loving dog, Bleu. More examples of Geoffrey's diverse and captivating work can be found at www.geoffreymundon.com.